Canticles and
Gathering Prayers

Canticles and Gathering Prayers

Prayers Compiled by John P. Mossi

Songs by Suzanne Toolan

Saint Mary's Press
Christian Brothers Publications
Winona, Minnesota

IMPRIMI POTEST
John W. Clark, SJ
Provincial

The publishing team included Carl Koch, FSC, development editor; Rita Rae Kramer, manuscript editor; Holly Storkel, typesetter; Elaine Kohner, illustrator; pre-press, printing, and binding by the graphics division of Saint Mary's Press.

Printed in the United States of America

Printing: 8 7 6 5 4 3 2

Year: 1996 95 94 93 92 91 90

ISBN 0-88489-228-X

Dedication

*To those who believe
that in Christ
there is neither
Gentile nor Jew,
servant nor free,
woman nor man,
but One Bread,
One Cup,
One Body*

Contents

Fraction Rites

Foreword

Canticles and Gathering Prayers is a welcome resource for the Christian community at prayer. Using a variety of prayer forms, Christian communities have always gathered to pray and celebrate, but several contemporary movements are changing the ways in which we pray.

The ecumenical movement following the Second Vatican Council has brought about a spirit of cooperation and collaboration at the grass-roots level. Local churches frequently work together to address the urgent needs of poor and oppressed people. Specific issues such as sanctuary for refugees, the nuclear arms buildup, and the plight of homeless people bring together groups who respond from religious commitments and who pray together as an integral part of their work.

The retreat movement has also embraced an ecumenical perspective. Spirituality programs and retreat centers usually welcome all who seek God.

The ecumenical community at Taize, France, has responded to the spiritual hunger of thousands of such seekers by developing a unique prayer form composed of brief prayers, readings, and simple chants sung in various languages. The prayer of Taize emerges from the silence of an assembled community and gives voice to their longings and desires. The prayer of Taize invites belief and unites the community in its common search while always respecting the level of faith and commitment of individuals.

The chants in this volume have been composed by Suzanne Toolan after the style of Taize prayer. These chants can either taper off into a meditative silence or be used as a community acclamation punctuating a gathering prayer.

The Christian feminist movement is another major experience that is changing the way we pray. The use of inclusive language that honors the feminine as explicitly as the masculine in the way we talk about one another is an increasingly urgent matter in praying communities. The language and metaphors we use in addressing God should no longer be exclusively masculine. Women and men who wish to pray within the Christian tradition in a way that honors this fuller perception of God will welcome this volume as a creative resource on liberating prayer. Many of the canticles and prayers incorporate biblical metaphors that have been neglected—especially those comparisons that include the feminine names and qualities of God as well as the feminine experience of those who pray.

Finally, these prayers and chants reflect Christian communities' need for forms of prayer that emerge from community members and that are led by lay persons. The emergence of lay persons who have embraced Christian ministry creates a need for new ways of gathering people at prayer and of celebrating important events. Many communities pray under lay leadership and give expression to a wider variety of experiences than they would in exclusively sacramental forms of public worship.

The gathering prayers in this book invite us to celebrate events in nature—the seasons, the earth, and the natural times of prayer in the morning and the evening. They invite us to bring our needs into our prayer—our need for healing, for grieving, for intimacy, and for expressing our weariness on life's journey. They suggest that we pray as communities about our joint tasks—prayers for beginning a work, creating a community, and pursuing justice.

The fraction rites emphasize the sacredness of sharing all meals. The fraction rituals include scriptural texts, acclamations, blessing prayers, and ritual actions.

Not only does this volume encourage us to celebrate a rich variety of occasions for prayer—it also invites us to develop our own rituals. The presider can use these prayers as starting points and expand them with readings and ritual actions appropriate to the specific occasion and gifts of the community.

Janet Ruffing, SM
Fordham University

*P*reface

The prayers in this book are the creative expression of many contributors who shared their poetic skills and faith experience.

Special recognition and thanks are due to the following contributors: Jean Gill for "Mother God" and "Potter and Clay"; Andrew Utiger for "Cosmos," "Intimacy," "Tears," and "Serenity"; Marie-Eloise Rosenblatt, RSM, for "Come to Me," "Credo," "Evensong," and "Many Grains"; Kathleen Denison for "Inner Healing"; Janet Ruffing, SM, for "Wisdom," "Holy Spirit," "Wedding Anniversary," and "Anointing"; Kathi Mayer, SM, and Eileen Sanchez for "Full Moon"; the Reverend Charles Price for "Spring," "Justice," and "Pentecost"; Tom Hidding, SJ, for "Arise," "Gathered in Love," and "Sisters and Brothers." It was my joy to compose the remaining prayers and to compile the book. Suzanne Toolan, SM, composed each of the canticles.

Many other friends have supported the genesis of *Canticles and Gathering Prayers*. Such encouragement and yearning for the development of new worship forms that are respectful of women's issues, inclusive language, feminine metaphors, and a more shared liturgical dynamic has spurred our work.

Finally, Suzanne and I would like to thank our communities—Mercy Center of Burlingame, and Jesuit Retreat House of Los Altos—for their reassuring support.

John Mossi, SJ

*I*ntroduction

Worship is an inherent component of the human journey. Whether in private or assembled, people pray to their God. In orchestrated, liturgical, and communal settings, people gather, dance, tell stories, sing, listen to holy writings, enter into periods of silence, and perhaps offer sacrifice, praise, thanksgiving, and intercessions to the Source of Life.

From the time of the early Church, women and men have gathered to reflect upon the sacred Scriptures, sing hymns, exchange the sign of peace, break bread, acclaim the Paschal Mystery, and give praise and thanks for the saving actions of the Creator, Redeemer, and Sanctifier.

Faithful to the spirituality of the early Christians, *Canticles and Gathering Prayers* offers the ecumenical Christian community a collection of *canticles, gathering prayers,* and *fraction rites*. This resource can be used to plan and to worship when formal, church or sacramental settings are not readily available, appropriate, or desired.

The Components Explained

Canticles are short songs—usually of one line. One canticle is included as the responsorial verse to be sung or recited in each gathering prayer and fraction rite. However, the canticles may also be used as sung prayers, meditative mantras, litanies, poetry, or responses to scriptural or alternative readings.

The canticles have been arranged for keyboard and/or guitar. They are short, simple, and easily sung by groups of untrained singers. Practice the canticles with the gathering before your prayer service begins so that all members of the community can participate in the entire prayer.

Music has been an integral part of worship throughout history. It serves as a vehicle of communal prayer, as a way of expressing emotion, providing a means to linger over God's word, to elongate it, to interiorize it, and thereby to move people's heads, hearts, and wills. The adage "those who sing, pray twice" remains true. Sung prayer binds an assembly together. Songs give voice to festive joy or to plaintive sorrow in ways that are impossible with the spoken word.

The canticles can be sung outside structured, communal services. They can enliven those moments when you are involved in routine activities. Quietly singing one of the canticles can help you center and maintain peace in a traffic snarl, a supermarket line, a doctor's waiting room, or during those monotonous chores that must be done.

Gathering prayers are prayers of thanksgiving. Some are based on scriptural texts, some reflect the principal themes of creation and redemption, some are written for specific occasions. These prayers are intentionally non-sacramental in structure so that the liturgical expression and level of participation in the celebration may be as inclusive and ecumenical as possible.

Fraction rites are meal prayers for the sharing of bread, wine, or other food. The fraction prayers may be used at home, at congregational dinners, for banquets, or for community feasts as table blessings prior to meals. Most of the fraction prayers use the Scriptures as their principal source.

No presider is specified for the gathering prayers or fraction rites. A member of the community may act as presider to start the prayer or to offer the whole prayer, with the community joining in solely on the responses, or the community together may recite the entire prayer.

Using *Canticles and Gathering Prayers* in Worship

In designing your worship service begin by asking yourself, what is the purpose of the event to be celebrated? Once that is determined, choose the readings, songs, prayers, and ritual actions that will best reflect the theme and purpose of the service.

The canticles, gathering prayers, and fraction rites may each be used separately or combined. For example, you might sing one of the canticles repeatedly as a sung prayer during a community celebration. Or your group might use a gathering prayer in a service, but recite the canticle instead of singing it. Other readings or hymns may be added around the gathering prayer. Or you might begin a community prayer with a gathering prayer and continue with one of the fraction rites. In short, each of the three components of this book may be used in many combinations. **Note that several of the gathering prayers and fraction rites begin with an *italicized* paragraph of instructions to the leader, which is not to be read aloud as part of the responsorial.**

If in planning your gathering you need to adapt, shorten, or expand the proposed gathering prayers or fraction rites contained in this book, feel free to do so. Creativity, flexibility, and intuition are key ingredients of meaningful worship. These canticles and prayers are intended to help you meet your needs in worship.

Gathering Prayers:

Prayers of Friendship, Thanksgiving, and Praise

1: *Mother God*

Adapted from Psalms 22, 131, and 139

God, our Mother,
you embrace us in feminine ways.
Nurture your people
and hold us in your arms.

Response

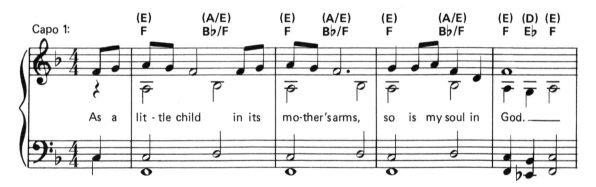

We give thanks to you, O God,
our good and loving Mother.

You have brought us to life;
you have surrounded us with tenderness and warmth,
like an infant in its mother's womb.

 **As a little child in its mother's arms,
so is my soul in God.**

You engulfed us in your love;
you protected us from harm.

You nourished us with your life;
you formed us in your image.

We felt the rhythmic beating of your heart
reassuring us of your constant presence.

As a little child in its mother's arms,
so is my soul in God.

You surrounded us with peace,
O good and gentle Mother;
you sheltered us from turmoil.

But then you disturbed us with your labor;
your urgent and unrelenting pangs of birth
pressed in on us from every side.

We were frightened in the upheaval,
lost in the tumult.
We looked for your peace, and found only fear;
we longed for your stillness, and felt only frenzy.

Then suddenly we were free;
the turmoil was ended.

Yet terror filled our hearts.

You were gone and we were alone;
your close and constant presence was nowhere to be felt.

We called out with a piercing cry:
"My God, my God, why have you abandoned us?"

And then you gathered us
into your strong and gentle arms.

We felt your comfort once again.

We felt your presence,
and our fear was gone.

 As a little child in its mother's arms,
so is my soul in God.

You gathered us unto yourself,
O strong and tender Mother;
you brought us close to your heart,
and we felt again your steady, throbbing presence.

Then we suffered a new anguish:
the pangs of hunger tugged at our souls.

We longed to be filled, to be nourished,
to be united with you again.

You touched us with the soft warmth of your breast,
you offered us the milk of your great love for us.

 As a little child in its mother's arms,
so is my soul in God.

We nursed eagerly at your breast like an infant;
we were filled with the warm, sweet milk
of your tender and abundant love.

You tenderly touched our face with your hand,
and your compassionate love spread
to the depths of our soul.

You looked upon our face,
and your joyful love filled our heart
almost to bursting.

We became one with you again,
slumbering blissfully at your breast,
filled with the joy of your presence,
the rapture of your touch.

 As a little child in its mother's arms,
so is my soul in God.

2: *Arise*

God of Easter hope,
dispel the many forms of darkness that we encounter.
Help us to walk boldly in your light.
Arise, let your glory shine forth.

Response

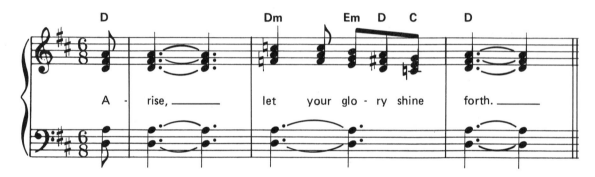

Arise, O people of God,
arise and shine forth,
for the glory of God is rising upon us!

Arise, O sleepers, see glory in our midst,
for God has come to make us a holy people!

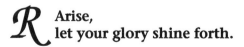 Arise,
let your glory shine forth.

Though darkness covers the earth,
though thick clouds quench the fire of our love,
you, O God, come to us in glory,
with brilliant light you pierce the dawn.

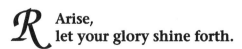 Arise,
let your glory shine forth.

Arise, O sleepers, from your despair,
for God will lift us high,
will give us the wings of eagles,
will show us the mountain of glorious delight.

R Arise,
let your glory shine forth.

Though the wicked may prosper,
and injustice threaten us on every side,
you bear us up in quiet mercy,
O God, source of all compassion.

R Arise,
let your glory shine forth.

Arise, O people dead with grief,
sadness will not haunt us forever,
for God is close to the brokenhearted,
as we draw close to one another in love.

R Arise,
let your glory shine forth.

Arise, O people of the light,
join hands and hearts this day,
that together we may find the God of promise,
the God that draws us together as one,
the God who is our glory forever and ever.

Amen!

R Arise,
let your glory shine forth.

3: *Cosmos*

Loving God,
all creation calls you blessed.
Your spirit imprints the whole universe
with life and mystery.
Yes, all creation proclaims your love.
We now join this chorus of praise.

Response

Loving God,
all of nature calls you blessed,
and so do we.

For you have woven an intimate tapestry
and called it life
and called it good.

From the darkest corners of the cosmos
to the sun-bright droplets of morning dew,
you dance the world into being.

Nothing that exists is apart from your love,
no song is sung unheard,
no death occurs unmourned.

In love you ride a dolphin's wave,
then turn to light a comet's tail.

 **Loving God, loving God,
all creation calls you blessed,
and so do we, and so do we.**

In love you have formed a universe
so diverse yet so related,
and into its web you call us forth
to walk the land and swim the sea
with all our natural brothers and sisters.

To the stars
we seem no more than blades of grass.

Yet to you, each of us,
as each blade of grass and each star,
is an irreplaceable treasure,
an essential companion on this journey of love.

 **Loving God, loving God,
all creation calls you blessed,
and so do we, and so do we.**

Gather us, God, into this creation
that we are so much a part of
and so much apart from.

We who are often blind to your presence
in the many shades of human skin,
need also to see your loving presence
in the spectrum of the seasons
and the colors of all creatures.

We who are often deaf to your presence
in the many creeds of human hearts,
need also to witness your loving presence
in the faith of the forests
and the creeds of sea and sky.

And we who are often too silent about your presence
in humans needlessly suffering in our world,
need also to cry out
that the compassion and justice
Jesus Christ came to teach us
goes far beyond our human domain.

 Loving God, loving God,
all creation calls you blessed,
and so do we, and so do we.

Loving God, as you lure the whole world into salvation,
guide us with your Spirit
that we might not be only pilgrims on the earth,
but pilgrims with the earth,
journeying home to you.

Open our hearts to understand
the intimate relationship that you have with all creation.

Only with this faith can we hope
that tomorrow's children will be able to end their prayer
as we do now
in Christ's name,
world without end.

Amen. Alleluia!

 Loving God, loving God,
all creation calls you blessed,
and so do we, and so do we.

4:   *Intimacy*

Passionate, loving Friend,
you are a God of relationships,
deep affections, and great trust.
You invite intimacy and communion.
The sanctuary of the heart is your dwelling place.

Response

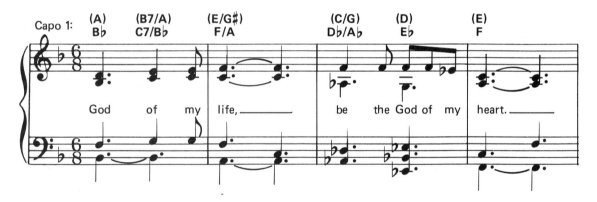

Blessed are you, O tender God.
You woo the universe,
count our every heartbeat,
taste our every tear.

You, dear God, are the lover we long for;
more passionate than any tempest
yet gentle as the breeze,
your love is as persistent as the dawn.

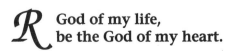 God of my life,
be the God of my heart.

No suffering of ours is without your sorrow,
no joy of ours is without the echo of your laugh.
Your patience awaits our every doubt,
your guidance beckons us in every darkness.

You, loving God, gently kiss our every moment,
as your touch caresses our weary body.
You anoint our struggles with your hope,
you dispel our blindness with your light.

 God of my life,
be the God of my heart.

God, without your intimate love we are barren,
like seed thrown on stones,
we are gardens without water,
candles with no flame.

Gather us to your breast
that we might find compassion.
In the quiet, hear the secret whispers of our life
that we might discover understanding.

 God of my life,
be the God of my heart.

Let your Spirit dance with us in the desert,
as with your beloved Jesus.
Woo us into justice,
seduce us into peace.

May your love, O God, ignite us,
that your song may greet us in the night
and your tenderness arise with us at break of day.
For as it is with Christ, so may it be with us.

 God of my life,
be the God of my heart.

5: *The Lowly*

Companion to the poor
and God of the lowly,
you extend compassion
to the powerless and to the forgotten.
Mercy is your name.
Help us minister with your concern and justice.

Response

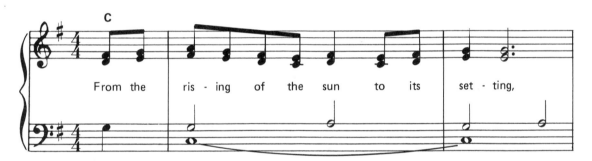

From the ris - ing of the sun to its set - ting,

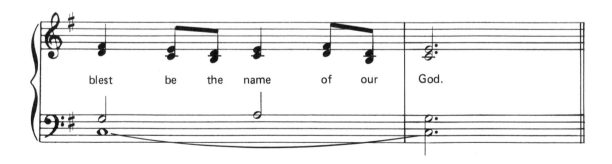

blest be the name of our God.

Praise, you servants of Yahweh,
praise the name of our God.

Blessed be the name of Yahweh
henceforth and forever.

From the rising of the sun to its setting,
the name of our God is praised.

 **From the rising of the sun to its setting,
blest be the name of our God.**

High above the nations is Yahweh;
the glory of our God transcends the heavens.

Who is like Yahweh,
enthroned on high,
watching the heavens and the earth below?

 **From the rising of the sun to its setting,
blest be the name of our God.**

Yahweh raises up the poor from the dust;
from the dunghill our God lifts up the needy
to seat them with rulers,
with the leaders of the people.

Yahweh enthrones the barren woman in her home
as the joyful mother of children.

 **From the rising of the sun to its setting,
blest be the name of our God.**

Extend your compassion to the poor people of our land.

Strengthen the unemployed people
and those hungering for respect and dignity.

Give courage
to victims of discrimination by race, creed, or sex,
and to those who labor longer hours for less pay.

Be a companion to our homeless persons
and to those who live in the shadows of our culture.

You are most merciful, Yahweh;
be present to your people in need.

 **From the rising of the sun to its setting,
blest be the name of our God.**

Stand by our elderly persons
as they face their latter years.

Be near the sick among us
who experience the daily loss of health and hope.

Especially be with those
who suffer from the isolation of AIDS,
who experience the fear, ignorance, and distance
of family and friends.

Yahweh, pour out your compassion
on all who minister to your poor children.

 **From the rising of the sun to its setting,
blest be the name of our God.**

Yahweh, we open our eyes.
Your poor ones are all around us,
in our cities and backyards, and in ourselves.

As you are not afraid to walk with us, your lowly,
may we, with Jesus, the Broken One,
serve the poor we encounter on the way.

 **From the rising of the sun to its setting,
blest be the name of our God.**

6: *Tears*

Gentle God,
comfort us in our loss.
Our tears are real,
they are tears of sorrow.
Stand by us as we cry out to you.

Response

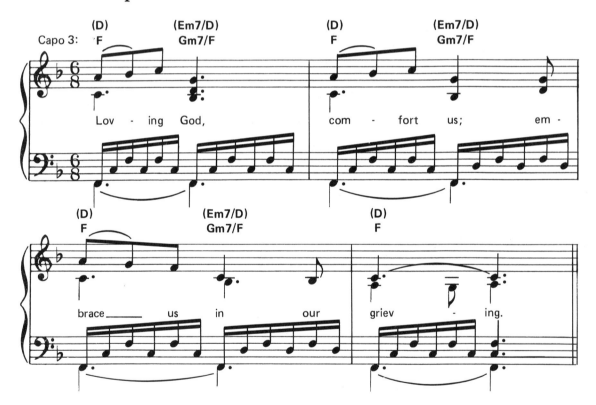

Beloved Creator,
we give you thanks for your love.

When we stand before birth and new life
such praise arises swiftly from within us
and slips easily from our tongues.

But when we find ourselves, as we do now,
encircled by death and loss,
gratitude and blessing choke in our hearts
as tears cloud our eyes
and sorrow makes confusion of understanding.

Gentle God, even as we stand in the shadow of your love,
we feel more in a place of shadows,
lacking light and warmth,
than in a place of love.

 Loving God, comfort us;
embrace us in our grieving.

Death has left us confused and sorrowful,
filling us with questions
that are as deeply mysterious as the oceans
and as unanswerable as the language of the stars.

These are not easy questions,
but ones of anger and grief.

Their taste is as bitter as gall,
their touch burns into our souls.

Like Mary and John, our questions are as dark
as those clouds that hung over the cross.

Like countless others
who have stood in the wake of death,
we have questions that throw us into the same despair
as the absence we now feel.

We join a multitude of others before us
who have wrestled with the "why" of painful loss
and the "where" of your caring presence.

 Loving God, comfort us;
embrace us in our grieving.

Help us, God, to realize
that we are not alone in our sorrow,
but mix our tears with yours.

You who embraced a crucified child
feel deeply the pain of this broken and battered world.

Keep vigil with us now.

 **Loving God, comfort us;
embrace us in our grieving.**

Tender God, accept our desperate heart,
filled with deepest sorrow.

As the emptiness of loss becomes
a cruel and heavy burden to carry,
help us to lighten the load.

As despair and anger become merciless taskmasters,
help us to ease our slavery.

As fear floods our waking and sleeping hours,
help us to find the peace of faith.

 **Loving God, comfort us;
embrace us in our grieving.**

Creator, grant us the courage
to journey through our grieving and our pain.

Grant us the faith to know
that tombs are not the last word
but that resurrection awaits us all.

In these dark times, send your Spirit
to heal our sadness and our anger
so that, like Christ,
we may begin to heal one another.

 **Loving God, comfort us;
embrace us in our grieving.**

7: *Gathered in Love*

Blessed are you, Loving God.
You are our wellspring and omega point.
Your Spirit binds us together
in respect, dignity, and service.
Gather our community together now and in the future.

Response

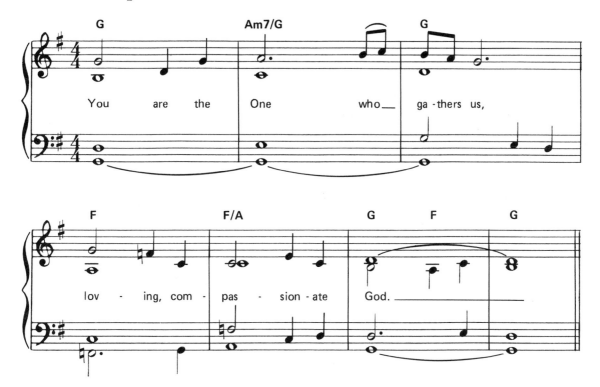

Blessed are you, Creator of All that is!
In your image we are made,
in your likeness you fashion and form us.

Your breath gives us life
that we may know you, O Creator.

Day by day you pour out your love to us,
that we might see the beauty of all you have done.

 **You are the One who gathers us,
loving, compassionate God.**

Blessed are you, Steadfast Lover!
You are ever faithful,
your promises endure through all generations.

Though we wander far from you,
your ardent desire to be our God ever calls us back.

With a love spilling over its bounds
you draw us to yourself.

 **You are the One who gathers us,
loving, compassionate God.**

Blessed are you, Gracious Giver of Salvation!
Your great power wells up within us
to be our strength,
to be our hope,
to be our glory.

With your mighty arms
you shelter us in times of distress.

You go before us
that with your grace we may win victory over death.

 **You are the One who gathers us,
loving, compassionate God.**

Blessed are you, Source of All Compassion!
You tremble as a mother giving birth.

For when we, your people, suffer in darkness,
you bring forth light and life.

The warmth of your love for us
melts away fear and sadness.
You bring to new birth the dawning child of mercy.

 **You are the One who gathers us,
loving, compassionate God.**

Gather us now into one holy union.
Give us the grace to look beyond all divisions.

Show us the oneness that we are called to be.

Guide us to the source of all community.
Infuse our hearts with one desire,
and bring us to the fullness of your one love!

 **You are the One who gathers us,
loving, compassionate God.**

In communion with our Savior, Jesus Christ,
and with the Holy Spirit,
who remains our guide,
we, your gathered people,
give you all praise,
all honor, and all glory,
for by your gracious love,
we are a holy people for all generations,
world without end.

Amen!

 **You are the One who gathers us,
loving, compassionate God.**

8: *Serenity*

Healing One,
we seek deliverance from our addictions,
those obvious and those most subtle.
Anoint us with your serenity,
for we desire to walk freely in peace.

Response

Loving God,
we want our lives back!
Ransom us from our fears;
rescue us from our illusions;
and redeem our hearts from the bondage of shame.
For somewhere along the way
we've misplaced our very selves
and tried to fill the void
with false hopes or no hopes
and we desire more than this!

 Healing One, breathe forth your Spirit,
that we may know your freedom and peace.

Come, Beloved, and guide us home.
For the strange lands of our escaping
do not ease our hunger.
Memories do not keep a safe distance,
and pain breaks every promise to depart.
You know the wounds of our idolatry,
you whose love keeps honest vigil in our soul.
We have tried as often to replace you
as to replace ourselves.

 Healing One, breathe forth your Spirit,
that we may know your freedom and peace.

Each of us is your promise
we find difficult to believe.
Each of us is your freedom
we're so eager to chain.
Each of us is your truth
we so often deny.
Each of us is your love
we're so frightened to embody.
For each of us is your gift
that shame has persuaded us not to unwrap.
We've listened to its painful lies.

 Healing One, breathe forth your Spirit,
that we may know your freedom and peace.

Healing One, send forth the breath of your Spirit
to blow out the dust of our delusions
and fill our hollow hearts again with hope.
Recreate in us—*us*.
For we ask to be nothing else
than that lover you once lured into life.
Embrace us with honesty,
comfort us with understanding,
shelter us with serenity,
and welcome us back home to ourselves
and to you.

 **Healing One, breathe forth your Spirit,
that we may know your freedom and peace.**

9: *Prayer of Ezra*

Gracious God,
bring back your people from exile,
from the bleakness of desert wanderings.
As you are near to us in joyous times,
faithfully guide us through our trials.

Response

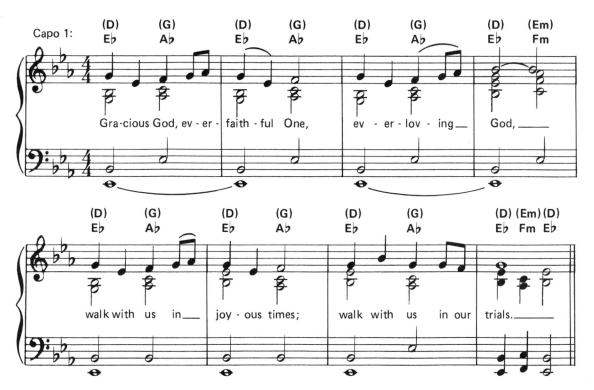

Nehemiah 9:5–15

"... Blessed are you, Yahweh, our God
from everlasting to everlasting ...!"

Gracious God, ever-faithful One, ever-loving God,
walk with us in our joyous times; walk with us in our trials.

> "You, Yahweh, are the one, only Yahweh,
> you have created the heavens,
> the heaven of heavens and all their array,
> the earth and all it bears,
> the seas and all they hold.
> To all of them you give life,
> and the array of heaven worships you."

 Gracious God, ever-faithful One, ever-loving God,
walk with us in our joyous times; walk with us in our trials.

Yahweh, you chose our ancestors,
and brought Sarah and Abraham out from Ur of Chaldea.

> "Finding [Abraham's] heart was faithful to you,
> you made a covenant with him,
> to give the [Promised Land to your posterity].
> And you have made good your promises,
> for you are upright, [as true as your word]."

 Gracious God, ever-faithful One, ever-loving God,
walk with us in our joyous times; walk with us in our trials.

> "You saw the distress of our ancestors in Egypt,
> you heard their cry by the Sea of Reeds.
> You displayed signs and wonders against Pharaoh,
>
> .   .   .   .
>
> for you knew how arrogantly they treated them.
> You won a reputation which you keep to this day."

 Gracious God, ever-faithful One, ever-loving God,
walk with us in our joyous times; walk with us in our trials.

> "You opened up the sea in front of them:
> they walked on dry ground right through the sea.
> Into the depths you hurled their pursuers
> like a stone into the raging waters.
> With a pillar of cloud you led them by day,
> with a pillar of fire by night:
> to light the way ahead of them. . . ."

Gracious God, ever-faithful One, ever-loving God,
walk with us in our joyous times; walk with us in our trials.

> "You came down on Mount Sinai
> and spoke with them from heaven;
> you gave them right rules, reliable laws,
> good statutes and commandments;
> you revealed your holy Sabbath to them. . . ."

 Gracious God, ever-faithful One, ever-loving God,
walk with us in our joyous times; walk with us in our trials.

> "For their hunger you gave them bread from heaven,
> for their thirst you brought them water out of a rock,
> and you told them to go in and take possession of the country
> which you had sworn to give them."

 Gracious God, ever-faithful One, ever-loving God,
walk with us in our joyous times; walk with us in our trials.

Yahweh, just as you were faithful in the past,
bestow your compassion and graciousness upon us
in our present journeys of liberation.

You indeed are rich in mercy and love.
Be with us in our struggles against slavery.

Send us wise and courageous women and men
to help us cross through our own seas and deserts.

Send, too, the gifts of your Holy Spirit
to protect us from the oppressive heat of the day
and to illumine our imagination and our way at night.

Gracious God, ever-faithful One, ever-loving God,
walk with us in our joyous times; walk with us in our trials.

Let the winds of the Spirit move us
as, on Pentecost, they inspired
the women and men of the early Church.

Like the prophets, apostles, and saints,
send us forth to speak your word and do your will.

We are grateful that as Friend and Spirit
you journey with us on our pilgrimage.

Blessed be your fidelity and glorious name forever.

 Gracious God, ever-faithful One, ever-loving God,
walk with us in our joyous times; walk with us in our trials.

10: *S*isters and Brothers

Adapted from Luke 11:28

Gracious Jesus, you are the revealed Word of God,
the Way, the Truth, and the Life.
You told us,
"Blest are they who hear the word of God and keep it."
In your kindness, walk lovingly with us this day.

Response

Blessed are we, sisters and brothers,
who praise the name of Jesus!

Blessed are we
who call on the Savior with one voice!

O Creator most sublime,
you sent your Word among us,
a Word spoken in the midst of anguish and despair,
a Word given as a pure and gracious gift.

Blessed are we who call on Jesus,
the Word who wipes away every tear.

 Gracious Jesus, walk with us this day;
gracious Jesus, walk with us this day.

Blessed are we, sisters and brothers,
who dare to call Jesus our brother.

Blessed are we
who walk together with our Savior.

All loving God, Jesus called you Abba
and showed us the way to you,
a way of tenderness and mercy,
a path of justice and truth.

Blessed are we, sisters and brothers of Jesus,
who now join hands in mutual love.

 Gracious Jesus, walk with us this day;
gracious Jesus, walk with us this day.

Blessed are we, sisters and brothers,
who embrace the hardships and pain of the world.

Blessed are we
who share the way of Christ crucified.

God of the brokenhearted,
you share the anguish of a people bowed down,
a people who have lost their way to you,
a people in need of your healing touch.

Blessed are we, sufferers with Christ.
Jesus, send us your mercy,
and let us touch our world in love.

 Gracious Jesus, walk with us this day;
gracious Jesus, walk with us this day.

Blessed are we, sisters and brothers,
who give voice to the glory of Jesus!

Blessed are we
who enter your gates with songs of praise.

God of glory and majesty,
you call us to rise from our sleep,
to open our eyes to faith in Christ,
to see the risen Jesus in endless light!

Blessed are we who gather
to praise and thank our God,
the God who is,
who was,
and who will be
forever and ever.

Amen! Alleluia!

 **Gracious Jesus, walk with us this day;
gracious Jesus, walk with us this day.**

11: A Chosen People

Adapted from Ephesians 1:3–14

Blessed be God
whose wisdom is beyond heaven and earth,
whose wisdom is Jesus the Anointed One,
whose wisdom adopts us as chosen persons
and seals us with the Holy Spirit.

Response

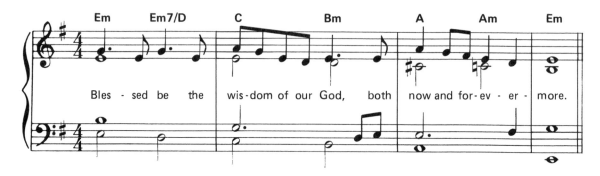

Blessed be God!
You have blessed us through Christ
with every spiritual blessing!

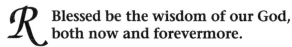 Blessed be the wisdom of our God,
both now and forevermore.

You chose us before Creation,
to be holy and blameless in your sight,
to be full of love.

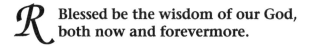 Blessed be the wisdom of our God,
both now and forevermore.

Likewise, you chose us through Jesus
to be Christ's adopted ones—

this was your pleasing intention—
that all might praise the divine favor
bestowed on us in the beloved.

 **Blessed be the wisdom of our God,
both now and forevermore.**

In Christ and through the blood of the cross
we are redeemed and our sins forgiven.
Without limits are your favors and gifts to us.

 **Blessed be the wisdom of our God,
both now and forevermore.**

God, you have bestowed the wisdom on us
to comprehend the mystery,
the plan you lovingly proclaimed in Christ
and brought to fruition in the fullness of time.
All of Creation, the heavens and the earth,
are brought together under the headship of Jesus the Christ.

 **Blessed be the wisdom of our God,
both now and forevermore.**

In Christ, our destiny was planned
according to your divine will.
We have been chosen to praise your glory.
We are a people who place all our hope in Christ.
For this were we formed in our mother's womb.

 **Blessed be the wisdom of our God,
both now and forevermore.**

In Christ we are now chosen;
for in hearing the glad tidings of salvation,
the word of truth,
and believing in it,
we are sealed with the Holy Spirit,
who is our promise, the pledge of our inheritance,
and who enables us
to praise you, our God.

 **Blessed be the wisdom of our God,
both now and forevermore.**

12: Potter and Clay

Let us attentively listen
to the inspiration of Saint Irenaeus.
Here we encounter God as the Artist-Potter
who desires to shape us
into beautiful earthen vessels:

It is not you who shape God;
it is God who shapes you.
If then you are the work of God,
await the hand of the Artist
who does all things in due season.
Offer the Potter your heart, soft and tractable,
and keep the form in which
the Artist has fashioned you.
Let your clay be moist,
lest you grow hard and lose
the imprint of the Potter's fingers.

(*Saint Irenaeus*)

Response

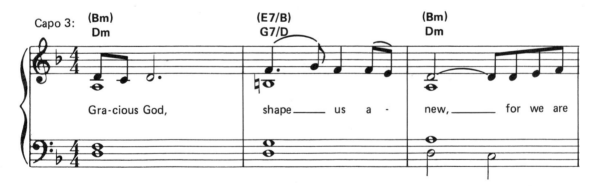

Capo 3:   (Bm)   (E7/B)   (Bm)
           Dm   G7/D   Dm

Gra-cious God,   shape ___ us a - new, ___   for we are

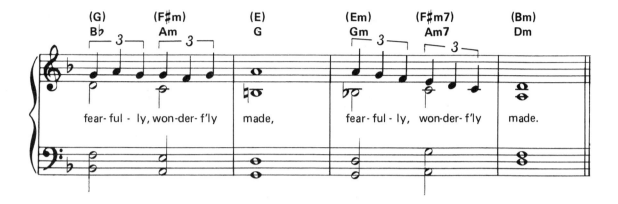

fear- ful - ly, won-der- f'ly made, fear- ful - ly, won-der- ly f'ly made.

Adapted from Jeremiah 18 and Psalm 139

We give you thanks, Yahweh,
for we are fearfully, wonderfully made.
Wonderful are your works.

You are the potter;
we are the clay,
the work of your hands.

You have touched us with your goodness.
You have made us in your image,
into your likeness you have shaped us.

 **Gracious God, shape us anew,
for we are fearfully, wonderfully made,
fearfully, wonderfully made.**

You have touched us, Yahweh,
and we have drawn back.

We have recoiled from your hand;
we have turned away in fear.

Yet you have waited,
waited for our return.

Then we found new courage,
and we turned again to you.

You received us into your hands,
enfolding us in your tender mercy,
caressing us with your gentle touch.

**Gracious God, shape us anew,
for we are fearfully, wonderfully made,
fearfully, wonderfully made.**

You have touched us, Yahweh,
and we have hardened ourselves away from you.

We have resisted your touch.
We have tried to shape ourselves,
and we have failed.

Yet you refused to leave us;
you did not remove your hand from us.

When we let our stubborn hearts melt,
we softened again to your touch.

 **Gracious God, shape us anew,
for we are fearfully, wonderfully made,
fearfully, wonderfully made.**

Yahweh, you shaped us anew.
You formed us into beauty
and grace and loveliness.

You touched us and made us whole,
showing us the depth of your love.

You made us holy,
looking upon us with wonder and awe.

In turn, we look upon ourselves
and see the imprint of your hand,
the shape of your Spirit,
the image of your face.

We praise you and give you thanks,
O good and gracious God.

 **Gracious God, shape us anew,
for we are fearfully, wonderfully made,
fearfully, wonderfully made.**

13: Spring

Christ, the glory of spring,
is risen and present.
In prayer and song
we echo the Alleluia
of Easter and eternal life.

Response

God of spring, our freedom and fresh hope,
you enkindle the sun after the death of winter.

You send the gentle rains
to renew the face of the earth.

Bring us new life in the life-giving warmth
of the approaching season.

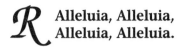 Alleluia, Alleluia,
Alleluia, Alleluia.

As you delivered your people at Passover,
make your servants strong in every age
to overcome tyranny,
to bring oppression to its end.

Bring us new life,
urging us to shape a free and peaceful world.

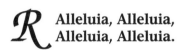 Alleluia, Alleluia,
Alleluia, Alleluia.

God, our Liberator,
you sent the Anointed One, who died our death,
and then you raised Jesus from the prison of the tomb.

Bring us new life
by the eternal strength
that comes through our Redeemer.

May we share the fulfillment of all joy
that the Resurrection promises.

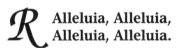 Alleluia, Alleluia,
Alleluia, Alleluia.

Faithful and Loving Friend,
all the signs of your compassionate presence
surround us here on this festival day.

We rejoice in the promise of your Spirit.

Our hearts thrill to the ancient words:
Christ is Risen!

Indeed the Anointed One is risen,
and lives in our hearts and in our lives.

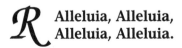 Alleluia, Alleluia,
Alleluia, Alleluia.

We give you thanks,
God of promise and of hope.

We believe that as you raised Jesus
from the bondage of death to new and everlasting life,
you will do the same for us.

Thus we cling, O God of Easter morning,
to your gracious promise
that we shall share in Christ's Resurrection.

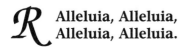 **Alleluia, Alleluia,
Alleluia, Alleluia.**

Send forth your nurturing Spirit.
Descend upon us as at Pentecost.

Kindle in us flames of understanding,
of patience, discernment, and compassionate concern
for the powerless and the forgotten.

May we use our talents and gifts in loving service
for the good of our neighbor and the poor,
our sisters and brothers in need.

We desire to be your people of spring,
of freedom, fresh hope, and resurrection.

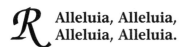 **Alleluia, Alleluia,
Alleluia, Alleluia.**

14: *A*ll Creation

Adapted from Psalm 148

Blessed are you, God of all creation
your sustaining spirit and love
animates the entire universe.
In gratitude, we praise
your life-giving energy and presence.

Response

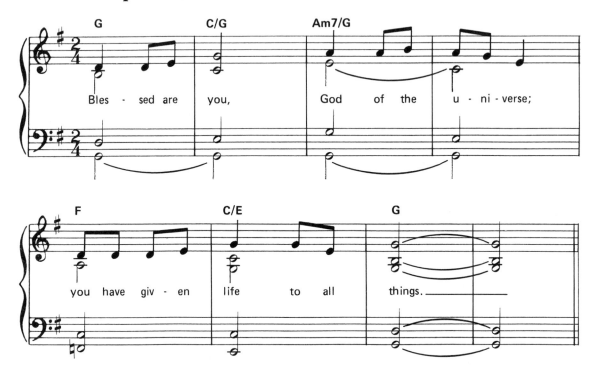

Praise God from the heavens,
praise God from the heights,
praise God, all you angels and hosts.

Praise God, sun and moon,
all you shining stars.

You highest heavens, you waters above the heavens,
praise Yahweh.

 **Blessed are you, God of the Universe;
you have given life to all things.**

Let everything praise the name of God,
for Yahweh commanded and they were created.

Yahweh established them forever and ever,
and gave them a duty which shall not pass away.

 **Blessed are you, God of the Universe;
you have given life to all things.**

Praise God from the earth,
you sea monsters and all depths;

fire and hail, snow and mist,
storm winds that fulfill God's word;

you mountains and all you hills,
you fruit trees and all you cedars;

you wild beasts and all tame animals,
you creeping things and you winged fowl.

 **Blessed are you, God of the Universe;
you have given life to all things.**

Let the rulers of the earth and all the peoples,
the leaders and all the judges of the earth,

young men too, and maidens,
the elderly, and boys and girls.

Praise the name of our God,
for Yahweh's name alone is exalted.

 **Blessed are you, God of the Universe;
you have given life to all things.**

Let all that exists and breathes
praise Yahweh.

The majesty of God is above earth and heaven,
Yahweh has raised the fortunes of the people.

May Yahweh be praised by all the faithful ones,
by the children of Israel,
the people close to Yahweh.

 Blessed are you, God of the Universe;
you have given life to all things.

15: Wisdom

Adapted from Wisdom 7 and Sirach 1

Come, Holy Wisdom.
Weave your mystery and profound gifts
into the fabric of our journey.
Come, Holy Spirit;
come, Holy Wisdom.

Response

Blessed are you,
gracious God,
in your Holy Wisdom.

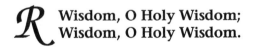
Wisdom, O Holy Wisdom;
Wisdom, O Holy Wisdom.

She is a breath of your spirit,
a pure effusion of your glory,
an untarnished mirror of your active power,
and an image of your goodness.

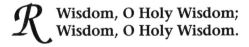
Wisdom, O Holy Wisdom;
Wisdom, O Holy Wisdom.

Artificer of all,
she knows your works
and was present when you made the world,
understanding what is pleasing to you
and in harmony with your desires.

Wisdom, O Holy Wisdom;
Wisdom, O Holy Wisdom.

Her delight is ever to be with us,
playing in and about the beauty of all Creation.

 Wisdom, O Holy Wisdom;
Wisdom, O Holy Wisdom.

You pour her forth upon every living thing,
and lavished her upon Jesus, our brother,
our hope.

 Wisdom, O Holy Wisdom;
Wisdom, O Holy Wisdom.

Send her forth that she might be
with us and work in us.

 Wisdom, O Holy Wisdom;
Wisdom, O Holy Wisdom.

Through her, enlighten our minds,
banish all fear and self-doubt,
and so fill our hearts
that we may think and speak truly.

 Wisdom, O Holy Wisdom;
Wisdom, O Holy Wisdom.

Make to yield before her gracious presence—
all darkness and confusion,
all withholding and domination,
all rigidity and fear,
all that is in us that works against
that which we are called to do today.

 Wisdom, O Holy Wisdom;
Wisdom, O Holy Wisdom.

May she dwell deep within us,
enfold us in her light,
imbue us with strength and purpose.

Wisdom, O Holy Wisdom;
Wisdom, O Holy Wisdom.

Above all,
may the doing of our work together
be one of the ways she fashions us
into members of the company of your
friends and prophets.

 Wisdom, O Holy Wisdom;
Wisdom, O Holy Wisdom.

May she hold us fast,
guide us in your ways,
and be our constant companion
today and forever.

Amen.

 Wisdom, O Holy Wisdom;
Wisdom, O Holy Wisdom.

16: Come to Me

Adapted from Matthew 11:28–30

Jesus welcomes us as we are,
burdened and weary.
Jesus graces us
with unconditional acceptance,
peaceful rest,
and a yoke that is easy and light.

Response

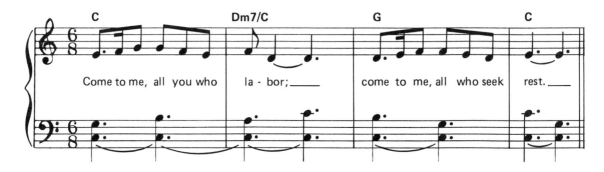

Restorer of the weary,
we call on you at the early hour of this day.

Share your life and spirit with us.

Nudge us out of darkness
into your own wonderful light.

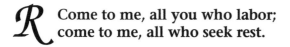 Come to me, all you who labor;
come to me, all who seek rest.

Instead of waiting until the sunset,
Love is the gift you give us,
at the beginning of the day.

You love us now,
unfinished as we are.

Though we are far from perfect,
you embrace us with unconditional love.

 **Come to me, all you who labor;
come to me, all who seek rest.**

For all we meet on today's journey,
empower us to love them as you love us.

Enlarge our hearts with your compassion.

Bend what is rigid in us,
relieve our confusion,
give us your wider, fresher vision.

 **Come to me, all you who labor;
come to me, all who seek rest.**

Do not depart from us,
but gently be our companion,
for we are in need of your reassuring presence.

Be with us today,
through our burdens and brokenness,
in the midst of tensions, challenges,
and the high expectations of others and of ourselves.

 **Come to me, all you who labor;
come to me, all who seek rest.**

The day is young.
Remain with us through each of its hours.

Let us hear your voice calling us anew,
restoring our energies
and willingness
to serve you with all our heart and strength.

 **Come to me, all you who labor;
come to me, all who seek rest.**

Call us again your apostles and disciples.

Here we are.

Send us.

 Come to me, all you who labor;
come to me, all who seek rest.

17: Justice

Blessed are the peacemakers.
Blessed are those who hunger and thirst for justice.
If we yearn for peace—
inside ourselves, in our community and the world,
we must work for justice.

Response

God of Justice, God of Struggle,
through the resurrection of Jesus
you delivered humankind
from the oppression of darkness,
from death and from sin.

You invite us to new life,
to freedom and joy.

 **Blessed are you, God of the Universe;
you have cast your fire on the earth.
Kindle it in our hearts, kindle it in our world.**

As your Spirit in Jesus
changed the course of salvation history,
encourage us
to transform those structures and institutions
that demean the dignity of your people,
especially the homeless, the poor, the untouchables,
those without power, without rights and representation.

 **Blessed are you, God of the Universe;
you have cast your fire on the earth.
Kindle it in our hearts, kindle it in our world.**

Deliver us from our false selves,
from our compulsions and unhealthy patterns
that keep us from enjoying to the full
the risen freedom that is our inheritance.

Deliver us from fear, hate, prejudice, greed,
and every desire to encroach upon our neighbor's life.

As your daughters and sons,
may we walk in the freedom of your light,
free in all our relationships with each other.

 **Blessed are you, God of the Universe;
you have cast your fire on the earth.
Kindle it in our hearts, kindle it in our world.**

Liberating and Loving Friend,
you sent Jesus to be our Just One and our Peace.

Help our hearts to rest in him,
especially when our peace is troubled by too many claims.

Strengthen us to work for justice as prudently as we can
and give us the humility to recognize our limitations.

Should we grow weak and weary in the struggle,
be at our side so that we may continue
in the footsteps of your prophets
who illumined the way to secure true justice.

 **Blessed are you, God of the Universe;
you have cast your fire on the earth.
Kindle it in our hearts, kindle it in our world.**

18: Full Moon

The inclusion of a basket of croissants, a pitcher of milk, a bowl of honey, a common blessing cup, and a candle-lit setting in the ritual can enhance the motif of Full Moon.

Adapted from Psalms 81 and 98

The moon radiates its fullness,
and sheds it soothing, caressing light.
Soft moonlight mediates the glaring sun of day
and the complete darkness of night.
Let us celebrate this festival of feminine light.

Response

God said, "Let there be lights in the vault of heaven to divide day from night, and let them indicate festivals, days and years. Let them be lights in the vault of heaven to shine on the earth." And so it was. God made the two great lights: the greater light to govern the day, the smaller light to govern the night, and the stars. God set them in the vault of heaven to shine on the earth, to govern the day and the night and to divide light from darkness. God saw that it was good. (Genesis 1:14–18)

 Blow the trumpet, blow the trumpet
at the full moon on our solemn feast.

. . . The city did not need the sun or the moon for light, since it was lit by the radiant glory of God, and the Lamb was a lighted torch for it. The nations will come to its light and the kings of the earth will bring it their treasures. Its gates will never be closed by day—and there will be no night there. (Revelation 21:23–25)

 Blow the trumpet, blow the trumpet
at the full moon on our solemn feast.

Feminine energy of our life-giving God,
shine the soothing light of your presence
on our lives this month.

Help us watch with expectancy
for those life-giving signs
we find it hard to see.

As we look for new signs,
new forms of your life and energy within us,
in song we raise our hearts to you:

 Blow the trumpet, blow the trumpet
at the full moon on our solemn feast.

Help us not to distinguish
between greater and lesser lights,
but rather to give thanks
for the light and for truth
wherever and however we experience them.

As we ask you to shed your light upon our earth,
we do so knowing that the greatest witness we can give
is our faithfulness to truth, and so we sing:

Blow the trumpet, blow the trumpet
at the full moon on our solemn feast.

We long for that day—the fullness of time—
when you alone will be all the light that we need.

Until that day comes, we give thanks
for tonight's full moon,
which "remains forever your faithful witness in the sky."

We pray that all nations may walk in peace
under the fullness of this light.

In a spirit of hope and reconciliation, we sing:

 Blow the trumpet, blow the trumpet
at the full moon on our solemn feast.

19: *Inner Healing*

Designed for a healing-of-memories service, this gathering prayer evokes the caring nearness of God. A meditative pause following each sung response is recommended.

Emmanuel, God-with-us,
we come to you this day,
seeking to be more aware of you in our lives.

Response

When we feel lost or confused
about the direction of our lives.

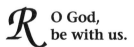 O God,
be with us.

When we sometimes feel
that we are journeying alone.

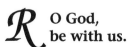 O God,
be with us.

When we forget
that someone is at hand
who knows and understands us.

℟ O God,
be with us.

God of our hearts,
healer of mind and body,
you are tender and compassionate,
slow to anger and most loving.

℟ O God,
be with us.

As we struggle
with our angers, fears, guilt, and anxieties.

℟ O God,
be with us.

As we seek your love to bind up our wounds.

℟ O God,
be with us.

When we are running away
from our pain and our fear.

℟ O God,
be with us.

God, you are near
to all who call upon you,
who call upon you in truth.

℟ O God,
be with us.

When we are afraid
to be honest in your presence.

℟ O God,
be with us.

When we feel you are far from us.

R O God,
be with us.

When the busyness of our lives
leaves little space to find you.

R O God,
be with us.

Companion God,
your presence is the source of life to us.

In you we live and move
and have our being.

Your love sustains,
creates, and redeems us.

Come then, O God,
and open our hearts,
so that we may find you within us—

Alive to what is hidden,
powerful in what is fragile,
loving in what is resistant to you.

Amen.

R O God,
be with us.

20: *Bless Yahweh*

As a celebration suggestion, each section of stanzas may be proclaimed by a different voice.

Adapted from Psalm 104

Bless Yahweh, O my soul.
How great you are, Yahweh, my God!

You are clothed in majesty and splendor,
wrapped in a robe of light!

Response

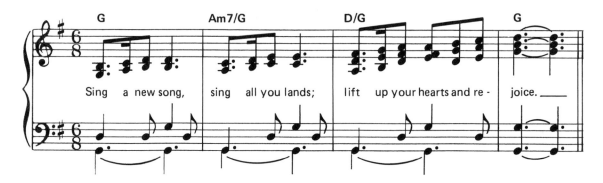

You spread the heavens out like a tent;
you build your high walls upon the waters above.

The clouds are your chariot
as you travel on the wings of the wind.

The breezes are your messengers
and fiery flames your servants.

 **Sing a new song, sing all you lands;
lift up your hearts and rejoice.**

You fixed the earth on its foundations
so that it cannot be moved.

You cover it with the deep as with a robe,
the waters enveloping the mountains.

At your charge the waters took to flight;
they fled at the sound of your thunder,
pouring over the mountains, settling into the valleys,
down to the place you made for them.

You set a limit they must never cross—
nor shall they flood the land again.

 Sing a new song, sing all you lands;
lift up your hearts and rejoice.

You set springs gushing in ravines,
flowing between the mountains,
giving drink to wild animals,
drawing the thirsty wild donkeys.

The birds of the air make their nests
and sing among the branches nearby.

From your palace you water the hills.
You fill the earth with the fruit of your works.

 Sing a new song, sing all you lands;
lift up your hearts and rejoice.

You make fresh grass grow for the cattle
and fruit for your people.

You bring forth food from the earth:
wine to make them rejoice,
oil to make them happy,
and bread to make them strong.

The trees of Yahweh are well watered—
those cedars of Lebanon.

Here the birds build their nest;
on the highest branches, the stork has its home.

For the wild goats there are the mountains;
badgers hide in the rocks.

 Sing a new song, sing all you lands;
lift up your hearts and rejoice.

You made the moon to mark the seasons;
the sun knows the hour of its setting.

You form the shadows, night falls,
and all the forest animals prowl about—

the lions roar for their prey
and seek their food from God.

At sunrise they retire,
to lie down in their lairs.

People go out to work
and to labor until the evening.

 Sing a new song, sing all you lands;
lift up your hearts and rejoice.

Yahweh, how many are the works you have created,
arranging everything in wisdom!

Earth is filled with creatures you have made:

see the vast ocean
teeming with countless creatures, great and small,
where ships go to and fro,
and Leviathan that you made to play for you.

 Sing a new song, sing all you lands;
lift up your hearts and rejoice.

All creatures depend on you
to give them food in due season.

You give the food they eat;
with generous hand, you fill them with good things.

If you turn your face away—they suffer;
if you stop their breath—they die and return to dust.

When you give your Spirit, they are created.
You keep renewing the world.

Glory forever to you, Yahweh!
May you find joy in your Creation.

 Sing a new song, sing all you lands;
lift up your hearts and rejoice.

21: *Holy Spirit*

Come, Holy Spirit,
animate our growth in justice.
Mend our brokenness so that we may be your peace.
Strengthen us with your gifts.
Come now, Blessed Spirit.

Response

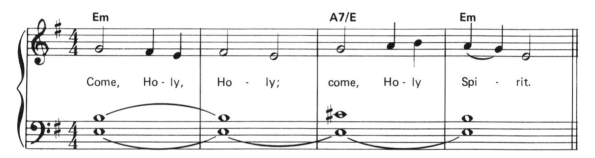

Come, Holy Spirit,
come fill our hearts with your love.
Surround us with the warmth of your presence.

℟ Come, Holy, Holy;
come, Holy Spirit.

Heal us and draw us close to our God.
Lead us across the great unknown,
the vast desert of uncertainty.

℟ Come, Holy, Holy;
come, Holy Spirit.

Come, Holy Spirit,
move in us and through us.
Bind up our wounds,
and draw us together into one body.

R Come, Holy, Holy;
come, Holy Spirit.

Drive out all darkness
that keeps us from love and from life.
Give us new eyes of faith,
a new voice of hope,
and a new heart for loving!

R Come, Holy, Holy;
come, Holy Spirit.

Come, Holy Spirit,
open our arms,
that we may embrace our world in love.

R Come, Holy, Holy;
come, Holy Spirit.

As Jesus opened his arms on the cross to save us all,
grace us too with arms willing to suffer
in order to rise in glory.

R Come, Holy, Holy;
come, Holy Spirit.

Come Holy Spirit,
come with the fire of your love.
Spark in us a white-hot passion for justice and peace.

R Come, Holy, Holy;
come, Holy Spirit.

Keep ever burning in us the light of Christ.
Sear our hearts with Christ's victory over death,
that we may burn as beacons of unending love.

R Come, Holy, Holy;
come, Holy Spirit.

Come Holy Spirit,
keep us one in the grace of community.
Engender in us a holy and mutual love,
a love shared among us.

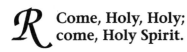 **Come, Holy, Holy;
come, Holy Spirit.**

Lead us always in your truth
that we might come to share
the glory which is ours
through Jesus Christ, our Risen Savior,
God forever and ever.

Amen!

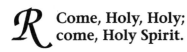 **Come, Holy, Holy;
come, Holy Spirit.**

22: Credo

As a people of faith,
let us profess
with union of hearts and voices
our belief in God—
Creator, Redeemer, and Sanctifier.

Response

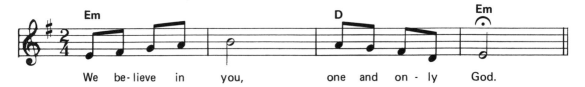

We believe in you, one and only God;
we take notice of all you have made
and find the cosmos wholesome, holy, and good.

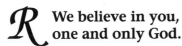 **We believe in you,
one and only God.**

We feel blessed in the truth you reveal
through Creation and word,
through women, men, and children,
through all you hold in store for us.

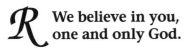 **We believe in you,
one and only God.**

We look to Jesus, living image of your love,
who was with you before yesterday began,
before the flourishing of this earth.

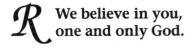 **We believe in you,
one and only God.**

Today you speak and act through the Risen One,
who is our Way, Fountain, Hope, and Justice.

 **We believe in you,
one and only God.**

Born of woman, Jesus is one of us,
drawing life from our life
and giving your spirit to us in fullness.

 **We believe in you,
one and only God.**

Embracing the fullness of humanity,
our Fellow Pilgrim has shared
our lot of disappointment, of weariness,
anxiety, and loss.

 **We believe in you,
one and only God.**

In pouring out his Spirit on Good Friday,
the Lamb of God passed through painful death
to radiant new life.

 **We believe in you,
one and only God.**

As Redeemer, Jesus Risen is with us
as loving presence,
as unfettered Spirit,
no longer bound by space and time.

 **We believe in you,
one and only God.**

We await the day when this new life and presence
will engulf us all,
when we will be with you
in this fuller life and larger sphere.

 **We believe in you,
one and only God.**

We believe that Jesus is, even now,
praying in our midst,
forgiving, healing, and renewing us.

 **We believe in you,
one and only God.**

We await the moment
when we will finally come home
to celebrate with you
and be reunited with the ones we love,
face to face
forever.

 **We believe in you,
one and only God.**

23: Pentecost

The length of this gathering prayer lends itself to a shared presidership. Each stanza is dedicated to a different dimension of God's presence. The interjection of appropriate poetry, scriptural readings, or ritual actions can further enhance the dynamics of the prayer.

Spirit of the living God,
come and breathe your life anew.
Passionate fire of Pentecost
ignite the talents and gifts
of everyone assembled here.

Response

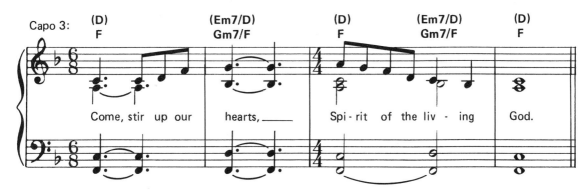

We praise you, Creative Spirit of God;
you hovered over the chaos
and moved over the face of the primeval deep.

By your hand the heavens and earth came into being.

Open our eyes to see
the creative possibilities of every situation.

No matter how painful or threatening
the chaos and opposition seem to be,
let us remember your Creative Spirit.

Come, stir up our hearts,
Spirit of the living God.

We praise you, Pilgrim Spirit of God.

In the days of our ancestors, you inspired leaders
like Sarah and Abraham, Miriam and Moses,
Ruth and Naomi, Jeremiah and Susanna,
David, Mary, and Elizabeth, [*add the names of other leaders*]
to lead your people closer to you.

You enabled them to bring victory from defeat
and abundant results from small beginnings,
for no obstacle can overcome your love.

Inspire us and our present-day leaders
to serve you without fear and to trust in your power.

Guide us, your pilgrim people
who seek your inspiration,
to new ways of working for peace and justice.

 Come, stir up our hearts,
Spirit of the living God.

We praise you, Uplifting Spirit of God.
You have enabled women and men to create
inspiring art, dance, and song.

Open our eyes to see and capture the inner reality
of your heart and soul implanted in the universe.

Open our ears to hear your silent music
so that in poetry we may imitate your heartbeat.

Sensitize us to the mysteries of the world around us
and to the awesome and glorious reality
of encountering you face to face.

 Come, stir up our hearts,
Spirit of the living God.

We praise you, Holy Spirit of the Most High.
You overshadowed Mary your servant
and blessed the child in her womb, Jesus,
as your Son and Word.

Overshadow us also
that we may know that same Jesus
as intimately and passionately as Mary did.

 Come, stir up our hearts,
Spirit of the living God.

We praise you, Loving Spirit of God.
You have placed love and joy and peace into the human heart.

Increase your Loving Spirit within us
that we may love our sisters and brothers with joy,
that we may forgive our enemies with understanding,
that we may become your ministers
of reconciliation in the world.

 Come, stir up our hearts,
Spirit of the living God.

We praise you, Spirit of God.

You guide us forward toward the heavenly Jerusalem
for which we deeply long.

Create in us a divine discontent,
an abiding hunger for fulfillment in your love.

Establish your new creation in us
so that God may be all in all.

 Come, stir up our hearts,
Spirit of the living God.

Come, Holy Spirit, come.

Come as the wind and stir our hearts.

Come as the rain and cleanse our souls.

Come as the fire and purify our spirits.

Strengthen, transform, and consecrate our life
so that we may praise you in all we say and do.

Come, Holy Spirit, come.

 Come, stir up our hearts,
Spirit of the living God.

24: Wedding Anniversary

Adapted from John 2:1–11

Loving and gracious God,
over and over again
you show us that you are a God of love.

At all times,
you are friend and companion to us.
Your joy is ever with us.

In your generosity
you invite us
to partake in the banquet of life,
to dance, to laugh
to eat the best of foods
and to celebrate your spirit and kindness.

Response

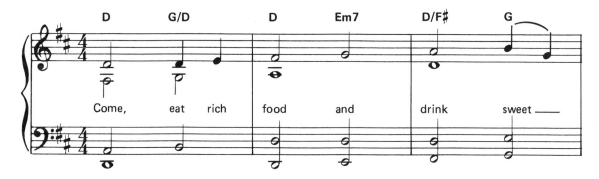

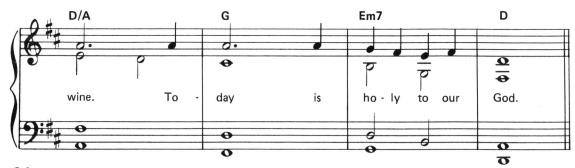

Today you are present with us
as we celebrate this wedding anniversary.

The sacred stories of our tradition
show your abiding interest and concern
in the human experience of marriage.

You made Eve and Adam to companion one another
and blessed them with all the good gifts of your creation.

You blessed Abraham and Sarah with the promise
of a child and a nation in their old age.

 **Come, eat rich food and drink sweet wine.
Today is holy to our God.**

Marriage, with its celebration and feasts,
continually reminds us
of the joy to which you invite us
when we live in harmony with one another and with you.

 **Come, eat rich food and drink sweet wine.
Today is holy to our God.**

In Cana many years ago,
Your Anointed One
graced the wedding of a poor couple.

Jesus showed himself to be at home at parties
and to cherish human joys and distresses.

Jesus' mother went to the wedding at Cana.
Jesus and his disciples
had likewise been invited to the celebration.

The wine supply ran out,
and Jesus' mother told him,
"They have no wine."

 **Come, eat rich food and drink sweet wine.
Today is holy to our God.**

Jesus changed water
into delicious wine.

The head waiter called the groom over
and remarked to him:

"People usually serve the choice wine first;
then when the guests have been drinking awhile,
a lesser vintage.
What you have done is keep the choice wine until now."

Jesus performed this first of his signs at Cana.
He revealed his power and love,
and his disciples believed in him.

 **Come, eat rich food and drink sweet wine.
Today is holy to our God.**

Gracious God,
even as we celebrate your glory among us,
we ask you to bless this gathering
of friends and family.

When we are reminded that life is short,
we desire even more that we may gain
wisdom of heart through the experiences life gives us.

Balance our afflictions with joy;
when you fill us with love through one another,
we shall celebrate all our days.

 **Come, eat rich food and drink sweet wine.
Today is holy to our God.**

Today, especially bless _____ and _____
as they celebrate their _____ wedding anniversary.

They have known the gift
of a good and happy marriage.

They enjoy the affection of their children
and continually praise you for your goodness.

Their lives have been rich,
full of good works and friendship.

During these mature years of their marriage,
bless them with health
and enable them to provide for all their needs.

May they enjoy many more years of each other's companionship
and may they know the fullness of your love for them.

Come, eat rich food and drink sweet wine.
Today is holy to our God.

Finally, we ask you to bless all here present
who share in this celebration.

May all of us find our way to you
in the fullness of love and friendship.

Bless this food that we enjoy
from your bounty and make us always mindful
of the needs of those who are poorer
than us in food and in friendship.

 Come, eat rich food and drink sweet wine.
Today is holy to our God.

25: Evensong

Evening is an appropriate time to gather and give thanks for the day. This prayer asks for peaceful rest during the night. Participants sitting in a circle and the use of candles and incense will enhance this prayer.

God of healing and rest,
at this day's end we come to you.

Lift us from the burdens of this day.

Response

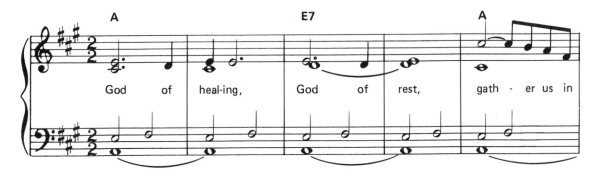

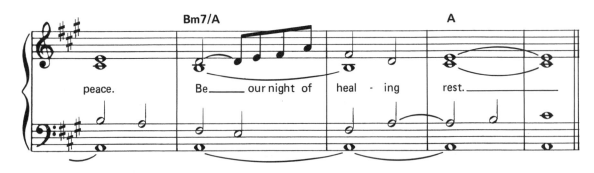

Your world is magnificent,
yet we forget to acknowledge your beauty
and the mystery of your inner workings.

Help us now to thank you
in the midst of our evening cares.

 God of healing, God of rest, gather us in peace.
Be our night of healing rest.

Make us again receivers of your life,
sharers of your gifts,
servants of you and one another,
and seekers of your wisdom.

 God of healing, God of rest, gather us in peace.
Be our night of healing rest.

Heal us at this evening hour
from diminishing energy,
from petty grievances,
from hopelessness,
from resentments,
and from our fears and jealousies.

Enable us again to seek you
in the beauty of our journey and our world.

 God of healing, God of rest, gather us in peace.
Be our night of healing rest.

Grant us wisdom
to listen to your voice
in our needed rest and dreams.

Give us courage to face you
in the quiet and stillness of the dark.

For you are as present in the night
as in the day.

 God of healing, God of rest, gather us in peace.
Be our night of healing rest.

As evening falls,
enshrine your hope and love
like a light within our heart.

As we patiently await your day of Final Coming,
be our Light unending
and night of healing rest.

 God of healing, God of rest, gather us in peace.
Be our night of healing rest.

Fraction Rites:

*Prayers for Breaking the Bread
and for Blessing Meals*

1: *The Feast*

As we bless this meal
let us pray to partake
in the nourishment of the Holy Spirit.

Response

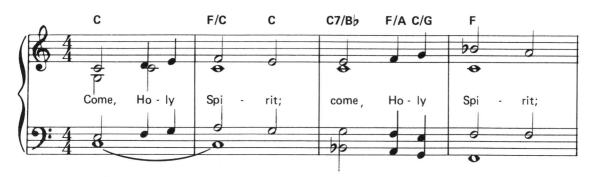

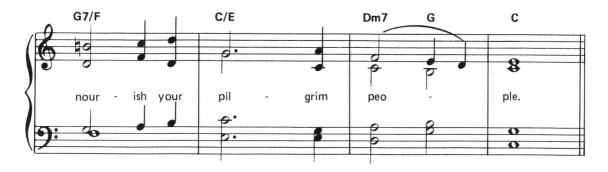

Adapted from Isaiah 55:1–3

All of you who are thirsty,
come to the water!
If you have not money, come,
I will give you bread to eat.

 Come, Holy Spirit; come, Holy Spirit;
nourish your pilgrim people.

Worry not about paying. For you, there is no cost.
Enjoy drinking wine or milk!
Why spend your money for what is not bread,
your hard-earned pay for what cannot satisfy your thirst?

 Come, Holy Spirit; come, Holy Spirit;
nourish your pilgrim people.

Attend to me, and you shall eat well.
Rich foods will delight you.
Come to me attentively.
Listen, that you may have the fullness of life.

 Come, Holy Spirit; come, Holy Spirit;
nourish your pilgrim people.

Come, take the bread and eat it.

 Come, Holy Spirit; come, Holy Spirit;
nourish your pilgrim people.

Delight in wine and milk.

 Come, Holy Spirit; come, Holy Spirit;
nourish your pilgrim people.

Listen, that you may have the fullness of life.

 Come, Holy Spirit; come, Holy Spirit;
nourish your pilgrim people.

Come, Holy Spirit,
sustain our hopes and desires.

 Come, Holy Spirit; come, Holy Spirit;
nourish your pilgrim people.

Holy Spirit,
be with us, your pilgrim people,
in our sharing of this simple meal.
As you nourish us with your gifts,
may we nourish one another
and those whom we are privileged to serve.

 **Come, Holy Spirit; come, Holy Spirit;
nourish your pilgrim people.**

2: *B*read of Justice

At the conclusion of this fraction rite, the prayer leader may distribute the meal to those gathered. During this sharing action, the response or other appropriate music may be sung.

Adapted from Micah 6:6–8 and Matthew 12:38–42

Justice and faith
comprise the liberating food of Christians.
With Jesus we pray
that our daily meal
may be the bread and wine of justice and freedom.

Response

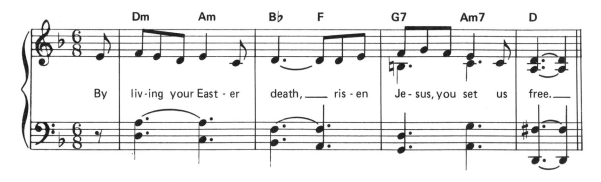

We now break your bread of justice
and prepare to share your wine of liberation.
Like the prophet Micah,
may we be mindful of the hungers and thirsts
of poor people.

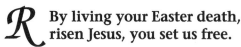 **By living your Easter death,
risen Jesus, you set us free.**

Our ancestors were freed
from the slavery and oppression of Egypt.
As we will soon partake of your manna of hope,

in the spirit of this meal may we
transform the present structures
that unjustly bind and oppress.

 **By living your Easter death,
risen Jesus, you set us free.**

Jesus, you are the sign of God's love and justice.
You are the broken bread of life, blood, and spirit poured.
May we, as your living signs of reconciliation,
walk in solidarity with people who are
broken, forgotten, and ignored.

 **By living your Easter death,
risen Jesus, you set us free.**

This bread of justice that we dare to break
is the new manna for our desert journey.
May we who are now strengthened at this table
labor in those institutions, governments, and churches
that are in need of the new manna and wine of Jesus.

 **By living your Easter death,
risen Jesus, you set us free.**

We pray, "Give us our daily bread."
This bread, freely given, costs greatly—
our spirit, mind, energy,
our feelings, soul, entire person,
all we have and are.

May we who participate in this sharing of life
seek the lost,
strengthen the weak,
and defend the poor.

Like Micah, like Jesus, may we
act justly,
love tenderly,
and walk humbly.

 **By living your Easter death,
risen Jesus, you set us free.**

3: *Martha and Mary*

Adapted from Luke 10:38–42

Martha, Mary, and Jesus,
assist us as we bless this friendship meal.
Show us the way
to balance the tensions of work and prayer.

Response

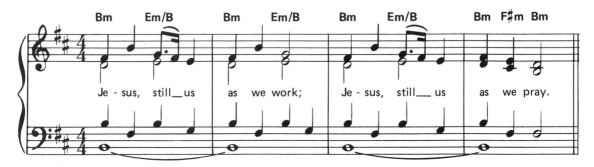

Je - sus, still__ us as we work; Je - sus, still__ us as we pray.

Jesus,
you entered the village of Martha and Mary.
In love and generosity,
Martha welcomed you to her home.
Like Martha,
may we extend kindness and hospitality.
May we welcome strangers,
pilgrims on their journeys,
and those who arrive in our neighborhood
weary and alone.
In your spirit, Jesus,
may we be humble and ready
to accept the invitation of Martha
to come and rest and dine.

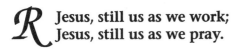 Jesus, still us as we work;
Jesus, still us as we pray.

Jesus, you received Mary's full, loving attention.
She had the gift to sit, to ponder, and to contemplate.
In our schedules, preoccupations, and agendas,
may we cherish and nurture these precious abilities:
gazing, listening, and being attentively present.

Help us learn from you how to
allow ourselves to recognize and affirm
the gifts in ourselves and other people.
At this meal and sharing time,
may we be present to one another.

R Jesus, still us as we work;
Jesus, still us as we pray.

Jesus, at your feet Mary listened to your teaching.
You said, "I have come that you may have joy to the full."
You abolished slavery
by calling us friends.
Where there was sickness,
you healed with your touch.
Where there was brokenness and sin,
you reconciled.

Where there was sorrow and affliction,
you blessed and soothed.
Where there was hunger and thirst,
you fed abundantly.
At this meal, may we be
your living good news for one another.

R Jesus, still us as we work;
Jesus, still us as we pray.

"Martha, Martha, you worry and fret about so many things."

Within us all, Martha lives.
With broom in one hand, duty and deadlines in the other,
we scurry about, preoccupied and frenzied.
We become judgmental, upset, and burned out.
We indulge in the self-pity of work addicts
and in irresponsible activity.

Martha, you complain
"Do you not care that my sister is leaving me
to do the serving all by myself?
Please tell her to help me."
Jesus, enable the Martha within us
to sit and to listen to you.

℟ Jesus, still us as we work;
Jesus, still us as we pray.

Jesus replied to Martha,
"Just one thing is really necessary.
It is Mary who has chosen the better part."
Help us to be calm, flexible, and hospitable.
Help us choose the role of Mary—the better part—
as we develop our relationship with you and your word.
Assist us also to know
the necessary part of Martha—
the importance of work—
and the difference between work and compulsion.
As community and friends,
may we not only work together as Marthas
but pray together as Marys.
May we blend work and prayer
this day and always.

℟ Jesus, still us as we work;
Jesus, still us as we pray.

With Martha, Mary, and Jesus
as our companions,
let us share this hospitality meal
in friendship and prayer.

℟ Jesus, still us as we work;
Jesus, still us as we pray.

4: Anointing

In the Gospel of Luke, the woman who anoints the feet of Jesus is a Christian symbol of the quality of intimacy that we are invited to share with Jesus and with one another.

The ritual action of this meal prayer uses anointing with oil as a sign of love and respect for all those present at the table.

A glass dish of perfumed oil should be placed in a position of prominence. At the end of the blessing, as the refrain is repeated, everyone may be anointed in a ritual way that best fits the group. Then the group may share bread and wine or a meal.

Response

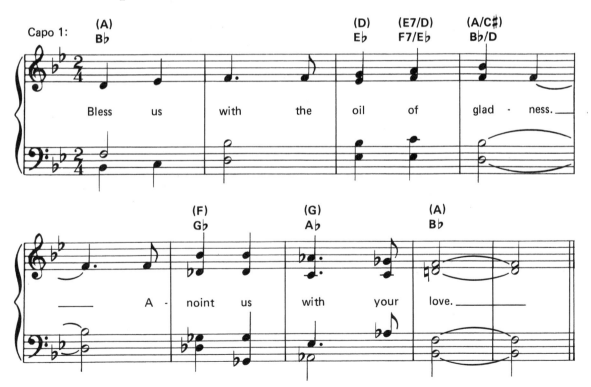

Luke 7:36–50

One of the Pharisees invited [Jesus] to a meal. When he arrived at the Pharisee's house and took his place at table, suddenly a woman came in, who had a bad name in the town. She had heard he was dining with the Pharisee and had brought with her an alabaster jar of ointment. She waited behind him at his feet, weeping, and her tears fell on his feet, and she wiped them away with her hair; then she covered his feet with kisses and anointed them with the ointment.

When the Pharisee who had invited him saw this, he said to himself, "If this man were a prophet, he would know who this woman is and what sort of person it is who is touching him and what a bad name she has."

 Bless us with the oil of gladness.
Anoint us with your love.

Then Jesus took him up and said, "Simon, I have something to say to you." He replied, "Say on, Master." [Jesus said,] "There was once a creditor who had two men in his debt; one owed him five hundred denarii, the other fifty. They were unable to pay, so he let them both off. Which of them will love him more?" Simon answered, "The one who was let off more, I suppose." Jesus said, "You are right."

 Bless us with the oil of gladness.
Anoint us with your love.

Then [Jesus] turned to the woman and said to Simon, "You see this woman? I came into your house, and you poured no water over my feet, but she has poured out her tears over my feet and wiped them away with her hair. You gave me no kiss, but she has been covering my feet with kisses ever since I came in. You did not anoint my head with oil, but she has anointed my feet with ointment. For this reason I tell you that her sins, many as they are, have been forgiven her, because she has shown such great love. It is someone who is forgiven little who shows little love."

 Bless us with the oil of gladness.
Anoint us with your love.

. . . [Jesus] said to the woman, "Your faith has saved you; go in peace."

Bless us with the oil of gladness.
Anoint us with your love.

Creator God,
you are the source of all life and joy.
Send the power of your Holy Spirit—
the Consoler, Strengthener, and Holy One—
upon us and upon this precious and fragrant oil
we are about to use.

 Bless us with the oil of gladness.
Anoint us with your love.

Bless this soothing and healing ointment.
Make it a sign of the strength and unconditional acceptance
that you extend to us on our journey.
May its fragrance remind us of your desire
to make us whole and healthy in mind and heart.
As you continually anoint us in your forgiveness and love,
may we anoint those we encounter along the way.

 Bless us with the oil of gladness.
Anoint us with your love.

Bless, too, this meal we are about to share
and all who gather at this table.
Anoint all our actions
and bind us together in loving acceptance and tender love.
We pray that our face will shine
with the oil of your gladness,
which represents the extravagance
of the love and joy that we share in Jesus,
your Anointed One and our Christ.

 Bless us with the oil of gladness.
Anoint us with your love.

5: Fasting

This table prayer, designed for the penitential seasons of the year, invites us to fast by developing concern for the plight of poor people. Sharing a simple meal of soup and bread would further enhance the impact of this fraction ritual.

Response

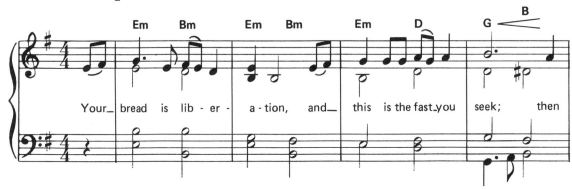

Your bread is lib - er - a - tion, and this is the fast you seek; then

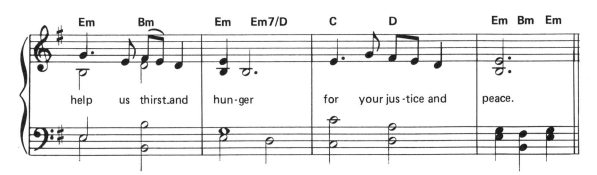

help us thirst and hun - ger for your jus - tice and peace.

Isaiah 58:6–11

[Yahweh speaks:]
Is not this the sort of fast that pleases me:
to break unjust fetters
and undo the thongs of the yoke,
to let the oppressed go free,
and to break all yokes?
Is it not sharing your food with the hungry,
and sheltering the homeless poor . . . ?

Your bread is liberation, and this is the fast you seek;
then help us hunger and thirst for your justice and peace.

> Then your light will blaze out like the dawn
> and your wound be quickly healed over.
> Saving justice for you will go ahead
> and Yahweh's glory come behind you.
> Then you will cry for help and Yahweh will answer;
> you will call and he will say, "I am here."

 Your bread is liberation, and this is the fast you seek;
then help us hunger and thirst for your justice and peace.

> If you do away with the yoke,
> the clenched fist and malicious words,
> if you deprive yourself for the hungry
> and satisfy the needs of the afflicted,
> your light will rise in the darkness,
> and your darkest hour will be like noon.

 Your bread is liberation, and this is the fast you seek;
then help us hunger and thirst for your justice and peace.

> Yahweh will always guide you,
> will satisfy your needs in the scorched land;
> [Yahweh] will give strength to your bones,
> and you will be like a watered garden,
> like a flowing spring
> whose waters never run dry.

 Your bread is liberation, and this is the fast you seek;
then help us hunger and thirst for your justice and peace.

> May we be your bread of liberation for others.
> Let your yeast of life, your flour of justice,
> and your water of kindness
> mix and rise in our imaginations and actions.

 Your bread is liberation, and this is the fast you seek;
then help us hunger and thirst for your justice and peace.

May we be leaven of living hope
for those who have little or no hope.
Inspire us to be your broken bread
and spirit outpoured
for our world and our sisters and brothers in need.

 **Your bread is liberation, and this is the fast you seek;
then help us hunger and thirst for your justice and peace.**

Mindful that we are called
to live generously and justly,
let us share in solidarity with one another
and with poor people
this ordinary meal
given to us by our God,
who is rich in mercy.

 **Your bread is liberation, and this is the fast you seek;
then help us hunger and thirst for your justice and peace.**

6: *Banquet*

O Wisdom, with graciousness and care,
you prepare a rich banquet for us.
In your abundant love,
all people are most welcome to come and dine.

Response

Proverbs 9:1–6

> Wisdom has built herself a house,
>> she has hewn her seven pillars,
> she has slaughtered her beasts, drawn her wine,
>> she has laid her table.

Wisdom, may we dine at your table
and share your goodness and love,
share your goodness and love.

She has despatched her maidservants
and proclaimed from the heights above the city,
"Who is simple? Let them come this way."

To the fool she says,
"Come and eat my bread,
drink the wine which I have drawn!"

 Wisdom, may we dine at your table
and share your goodness and love,
share your goodness and love.

"Come and eat my bread,
drink the wine which I have drawn!
Leave foolishness behind and you will live,
go forwards in the ways of perception."

 Wisdom, may we dine at your table
and share your goodness and love,
share your goodness and love.

Wisdom, in your goodness and love
we partake of your banquet of life.
We are not only grateful for this table
but also for the inner knowledge and spiritual ways
with which you nourish us.
Now strengthen our entire being.

 Wisdom, may we dine at your table
and share your goodness and love,
share your goodness and love.

7: The Journey

God of the journey,
as you accompanied and fed Elijah,
stand by us this day.
The journey is long and winding;
fortify us with your food and spirit.

Response

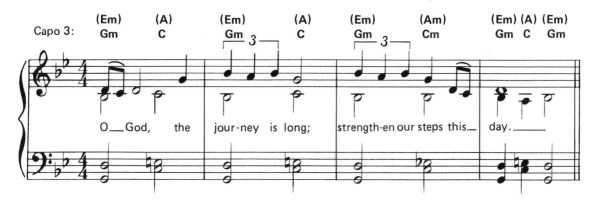

O—God, the jour-ney is long; strength-en our steps this— day.—

Adapted from 1 Kings 19:4–8

For a full day, Elijah fled into the desert wastes
and, coming to a furze tree, he threw himself beneath it.

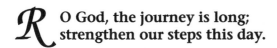 O God, the journey is long;
strengthen our steps this day.

Elijah wished that he were dead.
"Yahweh, I have had enough. Take my life!
I am a failure and no better than my ancestors."

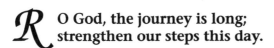 O God, the journey is long;
strengthen our steps this day.

Exhausted, Elijah lay down and fell into a deep sleep.
But an angel suddenly nudged Elijah, telling him,
"Elijah, wake up, on your feet. Eat what I have brought."
So the prophet ate a hearth cake and drank from a jug of water.
Then he slept again.

 O God, the journey is long;
strengthen our steps this day.

For a second time, the angel returned.
"Elijah, eat and drink once more.
Otherwise the journey will be too long for you."
Elijah did as he was commanded.

 O God, the journey is long;
strengthen our steps this day.

Fortified by the food and drink,
the prophet hiked for forty days and forty nights,
finally reaching Horeb, the mountain of God.

 O God, the journey is long;
strengthen our steps this day.

O God, the journey is indeed long
and our steps falter along the way.
At times, we become fatigued
as we encounter frustrations and opposition.
At times we, too, lose hope and direction.
We cry out, "Enough is enough. I've had it.
Go ahead and take my life."

 O God, the journey is long;
strengthen our steps this day.

On the journey, help us to accept
our human limitations, the limitations of other people,
and those structures that we desire to transform.
At the same time, may we not compromise
your prophetic invitations.
Grant us creative rest and deep peace of mind and heart.
Send your angels to touch our inner spirit

and to feed us with your nourishment.
Strengthen our steps this day.

 O God, the journey is long;
strengthen our steps this day.

Yes, the journey is long.
We cannot reach our destination alone.
Be our companion, just as you were to our ancestors.
Renew our vision and courage.
Stimulate our imagination
so that we may continue the journey—
not in isolation
but with your life-giving Spirit,
who is ever present
to nudge us with fresh inspiration
and quickenings of heart, mind, and body.

 O God, the journey is long;
strengthen our steps this day.

God of the journey,
your angels fed Elijah in the desert.
As we now break bread as family,
minister to us and our needs
so that we, in turn, can minister to others.

 O God, the journey is long;
strengthen our steps this day.

8: *Variety and Unity*

This fraction rite acknowledges that the diversity of gifts in the local community is a manifestation of the presence of the Holy Spirit. The participation of several prayer leaders—female and male, elderly and young—would further enhance this prayer.

Unifying Spirit,
bless and anoint this meal [us] with your charisms. [gifts]
Bring to fruition in each one of us
the diverse gifts that enrich this gathering.

Response

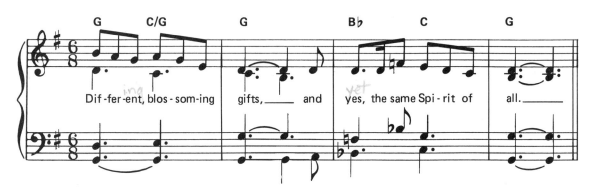

Dif-fer-ent, blos-som-ing [ing] gifts,____ and yes, [yet] the same Spi-rit of all.____

1 Corinthians 12:4–11:

> There are many different gifts,
> but it is always the same Spirit. . . .

℟ Different, blossoming gifts,
and yes, the same Spirit of all.

> . . . There are many different ways of serving,
> but it is always the same Lord. . . .

℟ Different, blossoming gifts,
and yes, the same Spirit of all.

There are many different forms of activity,
but in everybody it is the same God
who is at work in them all.

℟ Different, blossoming gifts,
and yes, the same Spirit of all.

The particular manifestation of the Spirit
granted to each one
is to be used for the general good.

℟ Different, blossoming gifts,
and yes, the same Spirit of all.

To one is given from the Spirit
the gift of utterance expressing wisdom;
to another the gift of utterance expressing knowledge,
in accordance with the same Spirit; . . .

℟ Different, blossoming gifts,
and yes, the same Spirit of all.

to another, faith, from the same Spirit;
and to another, the gifts of healing,
through this one Spirit; . . .

℟ Different, blossoming gifts,
and yes, the same Spirit of all.

to another, prophecy;
to another, the power of distinguishing spirits; . . .

℟ Different, blossoming gifts,
and yes, the same Spirit of all.

to one, the gift of different tongues
and to another, the interpretation of tongues. . . .

℟ Different, blossoming gifts,
and yes, the same Spirit of all.

But at work in all these is one and the same Spirit,
distributing them at will to each individual,
distributing them to each as the Spirit wills.

Different, blossoming gifts,
and yes, the same Spirit of all.

Holy Spirit,
we are grateful for the manifest ways
in which you reveal yourself and nurture your people.
As we break this one loaf, *As we are many sizes, ages, + personalities*
may we appreciate its many grains. *yet gathered into one worshiping community.*
And yes, may we appreciate the diverse gifts ~~and charisms~~
of those gathered here ~~for this meal.~~ *this morning.*

 Different, blossoming gifts,
and yes, the same Spirit of all.

9: *Called by Name*

This fraction rite concludes with the ritual of breaking off a piece of the loaf and handing it to the next person. Before each morsel is given, a brief blessing incorporating the person's name is prayed.

God, most intimate,
You are a God of closeness to our hearts.
You have implanted your likeness in us.
You know us each by name
and constantly send your love to support us on our way.

Response

O God,
your names are many and most tender:
Gentle One, Breath Within,
Holy Light, Gracious Spirit,
Womb of All, Keeper of Promises,
Enabling Friend, Amazing Grace,
Mystery of Love, Compassionate Heart,
Freedom of the Oppressed.
We praise you
and your many names
that reveal your constant kindness
to all who seek you.

 O most Holy God, we praise you,
for you have called us by name.

God of all seasons and all peoples,
we praise you because, throughout time,
you called women and men by their names
to be prophets, to lead your people,
and to be your living presence.
We especially give thanks
for the liberating name of Jesus.
As your angel called him
while Jesus was in Mary's womb,
so each of us is similarly called, known, and loved.

 O most Holy God, we praise you,
for you have called us by name.

Jesus called the disciples by their names
and sent them on their mission.
In the name of God
and in the name of Jesus
they healed the sick and forgave sins.
As the Risen One,
Jesus met Magdalene outside the tomb
and called her by name: "Mary."
Such is the way that we are called and loved.

 O most Holy God, we praise you,
for you have called us by name.

At this meal,
you reach out to each of us by name and as we are.
As Persistent Friend,
you call us in the deep recesses of our heart.
As Intimate One,
you dine with us.
As Breath of Life,
you live within us.
As you continually bless and love us,
bless our food and our time together.

 **O most Holy God, we praise you,
for you have called us by name.**

As you call us each by name,
may we call the name of one another
with affection and reverence.
As you accept and love us the way we are,
give us the wisdom and courage to do the same
for ourselves and for our sisters and brothers.

And let us begin now,
at this meal of union and thanksgiving.
As we break the one loaf,
let us break bread for one another,
calling one another by name
and blessing each other in prayer.

 **O most Holy God, we praise you,
for you have called us by name.**

10: *The Temptation*

Jesus, when you were tempted in the wilderness,
you reminded us that we do not live by bread alone,
"but by every word that comes forth
from the mouth of God."
As we prepare to eat this meal,
bless us with spiritual integrity
and a hunger for true bread,
the holy word of God.

Response

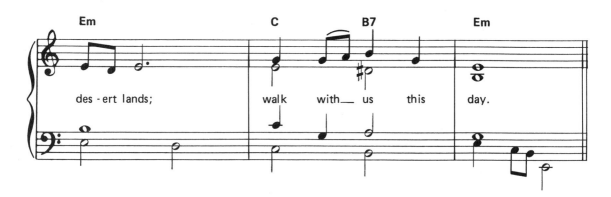

Luke 4:1–4

> Filled with the Holy Spirit,
> Jesus left the Jordan
> and was led by the Spirit into the desert,
> for forty days being put to the test by the devil.

 **Jesus, Jesus, walk with us in our desert lands;
walk with us this day.**

> During that time he ate nothing
> and at the end he was hungry.

 **Jesus, Jesus, walk with us in our desert lands;
walk with us this day.**

> Then the devil said to him,
> "If you are Son of God,
> tell this stone to turn into a loaf."

 **Jesus, Jesus, walk with us in our desert lands;
walk with us this day.**

> But Jesus replied,
> "Scripture says:
> Human beings live not on bread alone."

 **Jesus, Jesus, walk with us in our desert lands;
walk with us this day.**

Jesus, as we experience our own deserts,
and face the vulnerability
of hunger, weakness, and temptation,
send your discerning Spirit
to be our companion and to strengthen us.

 **Jesus, Jesus, walk with us in our desert lands;
walk with us this day.**

Walk with us as we face the shadow side
of our personal wilderness.
Assist us in extending your care and mercy to others
as they strive to walk through their deserts.

Jesus, Jesus, walk with us in our desert lands;
walk with us this day.

May we embody the holiness of your Spirit
to the lonely, homeless, and brokenhearted people
and to those who hunger and thirst for dignity.

 Jesus, Jesus, walk with us in our desert lands;
walk with us this day.

Seeking the true Bread of wisdom and courage,
we break bread and share this meal.
Help us to be sensitive to our various appetites
and inner voices.
May our deepest appetite and hunger always be
for your inspired word and Holy Spirit.

 Jesus, Jesus, walk with us in our desert lands;
walk with us this day.

11: *Second Class No More*

Adapted from Deuteronomy 10:17–19

Yahweh, your hand of compassion
rests on those who enjoy the least rights
and privileges of any class.
You call on us, your people,
to be your mercy to the poorest of the poor.

Response

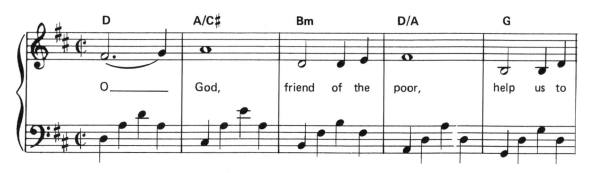

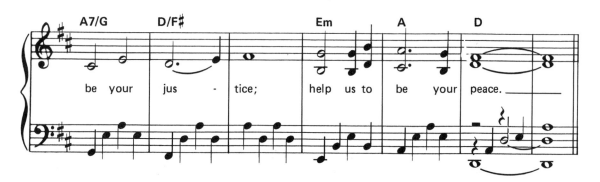

Yahweh, you are the God of gods,
next to you stands no other.
You are God most great and triumphant,
free of favoritism, never to be bribed.
Yahweh, you see that justice is done
for the orphan and the widow.
As your love gives food and clothing to strangers,
you remind us to love the stranger as well
for we were once foreigners in Egypt.

R O God, friend of the poor, help us to be your justice;
help us to be your peace.

Ephesians 2:19–22

. . . You are no longer aliens or foreign visitors;
you are fellow-citizens with the holy people of God
and part of God's household.

R O God, friend of the poor, help us to be your justice;
help us to be your peace.

You are built upon the foundations
of the apostles and prophets,
and Christ Jesus himself is the cornerstone.

R O God, friend of the poor, help us to be your justice;
help us to be your peace.

Every structure knit together in him
grows into a holy temple in the Lord;
and you too, in him, are being built up
into a dwelling-place of God in the Spirit.

R O God, friend of the poor, help us to be your justice;
help us to be your peace.

Your household embraces every nation and culture,
and extends to all women and men,
to the young and the old
of every race, language, and religion.
The temple of God is all peoples, the world.
May we reverently reach out to all people in justice and peace
so as to eliminate divisions and class distinctions.

 O God, friend of the poor, help us to be your justice;
help us to be your peace.

Let us also learn from strangers and poor people
new ways of seeing, living, and praying.
We ask for the boldness
to journey together as true sisters and brothers
of the one God who is God of all.
So we pray for the grace to work for justice
and to be your living sacraments of peace.

 O God, friend of the poor, help us to be your justice;
help us to be your peace.

We now sit down at this table;
let us strive to behold one another as God beholds us.
Let us be, with open hearts,
the justice and peace of God
at this blessed meal of life.

 O God, friend of the poor, help us to be your justice;
help us to be your peace.

12: Manna

Three readers may assist in this meal prayer, with each reader taking one of the main parts: Doubt, Manna, and the Call to Prayer.

Response

Adapted from Psalm 78

Doubt:
While in the desert, the people of Israel
rebelled against the Most High.
They willfully put God to the test
by demanding the food they craved.
They spoke against God, saying:
"Can God spread a table in the desert?"
When Moses struck the rock, water gushed out,
and streams flowed abundantly.
But can God also give us bread
and supply meat for the people?"

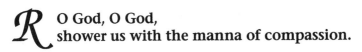 O God, O God,
shower us with the **manna of compassion.**

Manna:
Yahweh gave a command to the skies above
and opened the doors of the heavens;
God rained down manna for the people to eat
and gave them the bread of heaven.

 O God, O God,
shower us with the manna of compassion.

Manna:
They ate the bread of the mighty,
you sent them more than enough food to eat.
You stirred up the east wind from the heavens
and led forth the south wind by your power.
You rained meat down on them like dust,
birds like sand on the seashore.
You made birds fall inside their camp,
all around their tents.
They ate until they had more than enough,
for you had given them what they craved.

 O God, O God,
shower us with the manna of compassion.

Call to Prayer:
God of our pilgrimage,
you never cease to shower us
with your manna of compassion.
May we always be a people
mindful of your past and present
saving actions.

 O God, O God,
shower us with the manna of compassion.

Call to Prayer:
As a loving mother and a protecting father
you watched over the wandering Israelites.
So, likewise, watch over our journey.
As we break the gift of this bread
that nourishes our spirit,
as we share the gift of this wine
that gladdens our hearts,

may we be filled with abundant gratitude
for the countless ways in which
you bestow your love upon us.

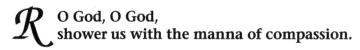 O God, O God,
shower us with the manna of compassion.

13: *The Body*

As the Body of Christ
we come together at this table of blessing
to celebrate our unity in God.
Let us listen to the word
so as to appreciate deeply
our interwoven dignity.

Response

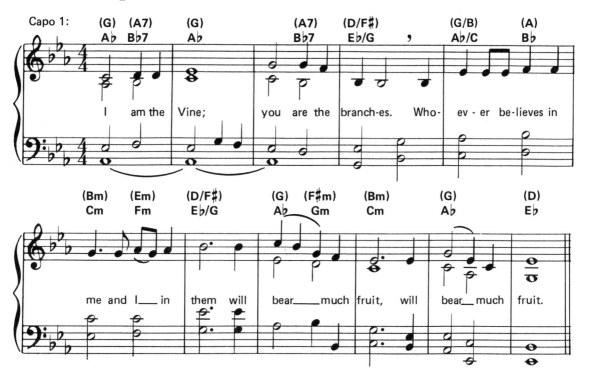

1 Corinthians 12:12–13

> . . . As with the human body which is a unity
> although it has many parts—
> all the parts of the body, though many,
> still making up one single body—
> so it is with Christ.

 I am the Vine; you are the branches.
Whoever believes in me and I in them
will bear much fruit, will bear much fruit.

> We were baptised into one body in a single Spirit,
> Jews as well as Greeks,
> slaves as well as free [people],
> and we were all given the same Spirit to drink.

 I am the Vine; you are the branches.
Whoever believes in me and I in them
will bear much fruit, will bear much fruit.

John 15:7

> If you remain in me
> and my words remain in you,
> you may ask for whatever you please
> and you will get it.

 I am the Vine; you are the branches.
Whoever believes in me and I in them
will bear much fruit, will bear much fruit.

John 15:11–15

> I have told you this
> so that my own joy may be in you
> and your joy be complete.
> This is my commandment:
> love one another,
> as I have loved you.
> No one can have greater love
> than to lay down his life for his friends.

 I am the Vine; you are the branches.
Whoever believes in me and I in them
will bear much fruit, will bear much fruit.

You are my friends,
if you do what I command you.
I shall no longer call you servants,
because a servant does not know
his master's business;
I call you friends. . . .

I am the Vine; you are the branches.
Whoever believes in me and I in them
will bear much fruit, will bear much fruit.

Jesus, you call us friends.
Dine with us at this friendship meal.
As you desire that we bear much fruit on the journey,
may we likewise acknowledge and build up
the talents, the dreams, and the gifts
of those assembled here at your table.

I am the Vine; you are the branches.
Whoever believes in me and I in them
will bear much fruit, will bear much fruit.

14: Bread of Life

As we lift up this one loaf,
we recall that Jesus is our Bread of Life,
an eternal manna
who alone satisfies our hunger.

Response

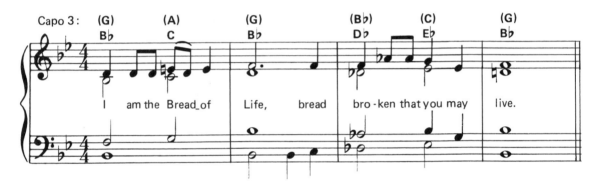

John 6:27–35

> Do not work for food that goes bad,
> but work for food that endures for eternal life. . . .

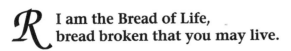 **I am the Bread of Life,
bread broken that you may live.**

> Then they said to him,
> "What must we do if we are to carry out God's work?"
> Jesus gave them this answer,
> "This is carrying out God's work:
> you must believe in the one he has sent." . . .

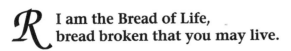 **I am the Bread of Life,
bread broken that you may live.**

The true bread . . .
the bread of God
is the bread which comes down from heaven
and gives life to the world.

R **I am the Bread of Life,**
bread broken that you may live.

". . . Give us that bread always.". . .

R **I am the Bread of Life,**
bread broken that you may live.

"I am the bread of life.
No one who comes to me will ever hunger;
no one who believes in me will ever thirst."

R **I am the Bread of Life,**
bread broken that you may live.

Jesus, we now break bread
and share this meal.
Give us the fullness of your Bread of Life.
Fill us with the freedom of your Spirit.
In imitation of your mission and the Gospel
may we be true manna for one another.

R **I am the Bread of Life,**
bread broken that you may live.

15: Beatitudes

This fraction rite celebrates the joy that Jesus said would come to people who live the spirituality of the Beatitudes.

Jesus, on the mountain side,
you multiplied loaves and fishes, healed the sick,
and preached the Beatitudes to the poor.
As we, gathered in your name, commence this meal,
bless us again with your words of beatitude.
May we truly be a joyful people who follow your path.

Response

Sustain the final note during the reading of the text.

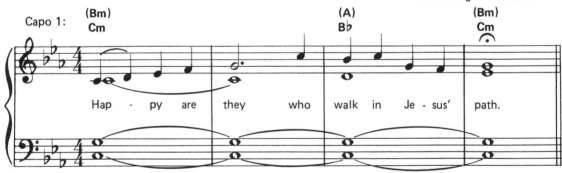

Hap - py are they who walk in Je - sus' path.

Matthew 5:3–12

How blessed are the poor in spirit:
the kingdom of Heaven is theirs.

℞ **Happy are they
who walk in Jesus' path.**

Blessed are the gentle:
they shall have the earth as inheritance.

℞ **Happy are they
who walk in Jesus' path.**

Blessed are those who mourn:
they shall be comforted.

R **Happy are they**
who walk in Jesus' path.

Blessed are those who hunger and thirst for uprightness:
they shall have their fill.

R **Happy are they**
who walk in Jesus' path.

Blessed are the merciful:
they shall have mercy shown them.

R **Happy are they**
who walk in Jesus' path.

Blessed are the pure in heart:
they shall see God.

R **Happy are they**
who walk in Jesus' path.

Blessed are the peacemakers:
they shall be recognised as children of God. . . .

R **Happy are they**
who walk in Jesus' path.

Blessed are you when people abuse you
and persecute you
and speak all kinds of calumny against you falsely
on my account.

R **Happy are they**
who walk in Jesus' path.

Rejoice and be glad,
for your reward will be great in heaven;
this is how they persecuted the prophets before you.

R **Happy are they**
who walk in Jesus' path.

Jesus, you are the Beatitudes of God,
sent to challenge and ennoble our spiritual path.
Bless this meal we share
and our entire journey with your Beatitudes.
May we be your peacemakers,
a people gentle in spirit, pure in heart,
and always full of your mercy.

 Happy are they
who walk in Jesus' path.

16: Daily Bread

Loving God,
you fed your wandering people in the desert
with manna from heaven.
Nourish us today at this meal
with your manna of mercy and love.

Response

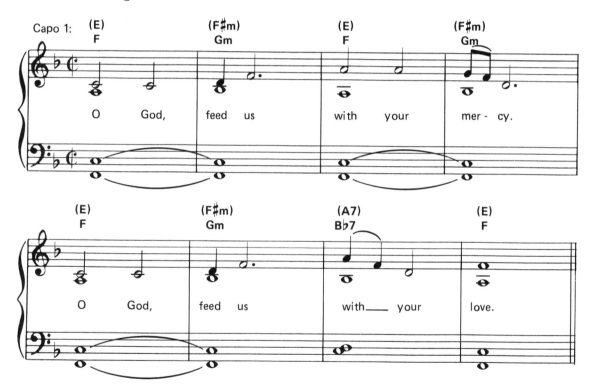

Exodus 16:4, 31–32

Yahweh . . . said to Moses,
"Look, I shall rain down bread for you from the heavens. . . ."

℟ O God, feed us with your mercy.
O God, feed us with your love.

"Each day the people must go out
and collect their ration for the day. . . ."

R O God, feed us with your mercy.
O God, feed us with your love.

The House of Israel named [the food] "manna."
It was like coriander seed;
it was white and its taste was like that of wafers made with honey.

R O God, feed us with your mercy.
O God, feed us with your love.

. . . "These are Yahweh's orders:
Fill a homer with [manna] and preserve it for your descendants,
so that they can see the bread on which
I fed you in the desert
when I brought you out of Egypt."

R O God, feed us with your mercy.
O God, feed us with your love.

Deuteronomy 8:3

. . . [Yahweh] fed you with manna
which neither you nor your ancestors had ever known,
to make you understand
that human beings live not on bread alone
but on every word that comes from the mouth of Yahweh.

R O God, feed us with your mercy.
O God, feed us with your love.

God, ever gracious and most bountiful,
continue to rain down manna on your people,
bless this meal with your spirit and word.
May this bread we break remind us
of the generous ways you fed your pilgrim people.
Kindly feed us today with your tender mercy and gentle love
so that we may be your mercy and love to others.

R O God, feed us with your mercy.
O God, feed us with your love.

17: Many Grains

Jesus, you are the Bread of Life.
In you we find our unity amidst diversity.
Through this meal and our prayer,
may we grow in deeper appreciation
of your risen presence, your word
and the countless ways that you invite us to fullness.

Response

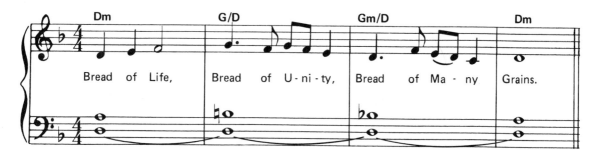

Bread of Life and Unity,
Bread of Many Grains,
proclaimed by faithful women and men,
preached through countless lives,
loved by the simple,
expounded by the wise,
handed on throughout the centuries;
Jesus, continue to be
our Life and Sustenance.

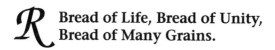 **Bread of Life, Bread of Unity,
Bread of Many Grains.**

Broken at different times,
in diverse settings and cultures,
the bread of your spirit and truth brings wholeness.
Your bread and life transform us
into your people.

 Bread of Life, Bread of Unity,
Bread of Many Grains.

Fashion our many grains again today
into a community for service of our neighbor.

 Bread of Life, Bread of Unity,
Bread of Many Grains.

As people of your bread and truth,
help us to hear the living word you are speaking,
the word that believers long ago heard
and faithfully handed on to us.

 Bread of Life, Bread of Unity,
Bread of Many Grains.

As we partake of this bread
and strive to break open the leaven of your word,
reopen our ears and hearts.
Give rebirth to our attentiveness
to hear again, as for the first time,
your word that brings the gift of life,
that binds us forever fast to you
and in relationship with one another.

 Bread of Life, Bread of Unity,
Bread of Many Grains.

18: Community

As we prepare to break bread together,
let us be reminded of the example
that the early Christians gave.

Response

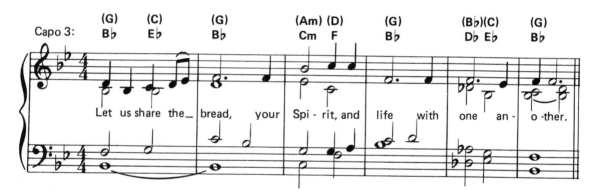

Acts 2:42–47

[The early Christian community]
remained faithful to the teachings of the apostles,
to the brotherhood,
to the breaking of the bread
and to the prayers.

℟ Let us share the bread, your Spirit,
and life with one another.

And everyone was filled with awe;
the apostles worked many signs and miracles.

℟ Let us share the bread, your Spirit,
and life with one another.

And all who shared the faith
owned everything in common;
they sold their goods and possessions
and distributed the proceeds among themselves
according to what each one needed.

℞ Let us share the bread, your Spirit,
and life with one another.

Each day, with one heart,
they regularly went to the Temple
but met in their houses for the breaking of bread;
they shared their food gladly and generously;
they praised God
and were looked up to by everyone.
Day by day the Lord added to their community. . . .

℞ Let us share the bread, your Spirit,
and life with one another.

Let us now share this bread
in the same spirit as the early Christians.
May it be a sign of our care
for one another and our faith.

℞ Let us share the bread, your Spirit,
and life with one another.

19: Passover

Four members of the community act in the celebration of this table prayer: a narrator, Jesus, and two disciples.

First Disciple:
As we prepare for our own shared meal,
may we be reminded of the ways
that Jesus, our new Passover,
feeds us in abundance.

John 6:2–13

Narrator:
. . . A large crowd followed [Jesus],
impressed by the signs he had done in curing the sick.
Jesus climbed the hillside
and sat down there with his disciples.
The time of the Jewish Passover was near.

Jesus:
. . . "Where can we buy some bread
for these people to eat?"

Narrator:
. . . [Jesus] knew exactly what he was going to do.
Philip answered,

First Disciple:
"Two hundred denarii would not buy enough
to give them a little piece each."

Second Disciple:
. . . "Here is a small boy with five barley loaves and two fish;
but what is that among so many?"

Jesus:
. . . "Make the people sit down.". . .

Narrator:
>Then Jesus took the loaves,
>gave thanks,
>and distributed them to those who were sitting there;
>he then did the same with the fish,
>distributing as much as they wanted.
>When they had eaten enough
>he said to the disciples,

Jesus:
>"Pick up the pieces left over,
>so that nothing is wasted."

Narrator:
>So they picked them up
>and filled twelve large baskets with scraps left over
>from the meal of five barley loaves.

First Disciple:
Jesus, just as you were present on the mountain side,
be with us now at this meal.
You are our Passover.
May we be your Passover people.
In your spirit and as your living signs
may we compassionately minister
to those who hunger
for food, understanding, and respect.

Second Disciple:
Jesus, as you took simple foods,
then blessed and shared them
with all the gathered people,
may we do the same.
As we now pass around this food and drink,
help us to nourish one another—
friends and strangers alike—
with your unconditional love
and bountiful generosity.

20: The Multiplication

In this blessing prayer for a meal, three members of the community may take the roles of Narrator, Jesus, and the Disciple.

Adapted from Matthew 15:32–38

Disciple:
Jesus often fed large crowds on the hillsides of Galilee.
He nourished them with the Beatitudes, compassion,
and multiplied bread for all to partake.
As we gather for this meal,
let us enter into the spirit of Jesus
who was able to multiply the goodness of God
for the people seated around him.

Narrator:
And now once again a great crowd had gathered,
and they had nothing to eat.
So Jesus called his disciples to him and said to them,

Jesus:
I feel sorry for all these people;
they have been with me for three days now
and have nothing to eat.
If I send them off home hungry they will collapse on the way;
some have come a great distance.

Disciple:
Where could anyone get these people
enough bread to eat in a deserted place?

Jesus:
How many loaves have you?

Disciple:
Seven.

Narrator:
Then he instructed the crowd to sit down on the ground,
and he took the seven loaves,
and after giving thanks
he broke them
and began handing them to his disciples to distribute;
and they distributed them among the crowd.
They had a few small fishes as well, and over these he said a
blessing and ordered them to be distributed too.
They ate as much as they wanted,
and they collected seven basketfuls of the scraps left over.
Now there had been about four thousand people.

Disciple:
In the spirit of Jesus
we pray that we may be a people of thanksgiving,
a people who share generously
the blessings we enjoy—our time,
                    our energies,
                    our talents and resources,
                    our compassion and love,
                    our food.

Narrator:
Jesus,
you demonstrate how to become
a life-giving sacrament for other people.
As we share this meal,
may we be instruments
of your peace and reconciliation
—especially to those people most in need of your touch.

Disciple
Let us now take this food,
lift it to heaven, break it, and share it,
knowing that this act is a promise that
we will love God and love our neighbors as ourselves.

*I*ndex

Canticles for Gathering Prayers

Canticles for Fraction Rites